Assad's Syria

Assad's Syria

Lara Kajs

Washington, D.C.

Assad's Syria
Lara Kajs
Published by Lara Kajs
1300 Pennsylvania Ave NW, Ste 190-320
Washington, DC 20004

Cover Photo: "Homs Airstrike 2012" by Lara Kajs

Dedication

For Brad

For the beautiful people of Syria.

To the millions who have made the most difficult decisions…

decisions that most of us will never have to make…

to survive.

May you one day laugh and smile again.

May your life and hearts be filled with hope, health, love, joy… and

peace.

Table of Contents

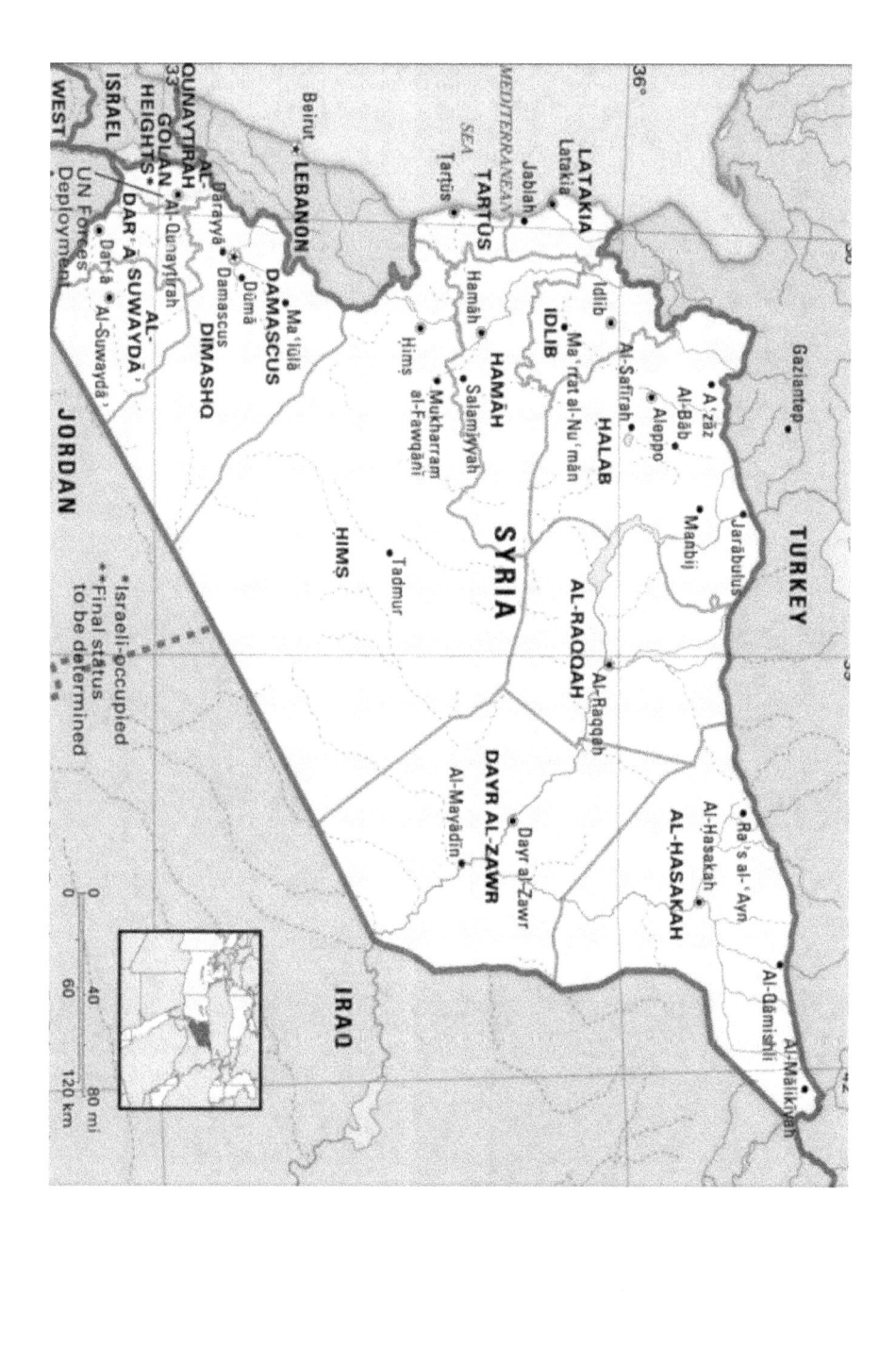

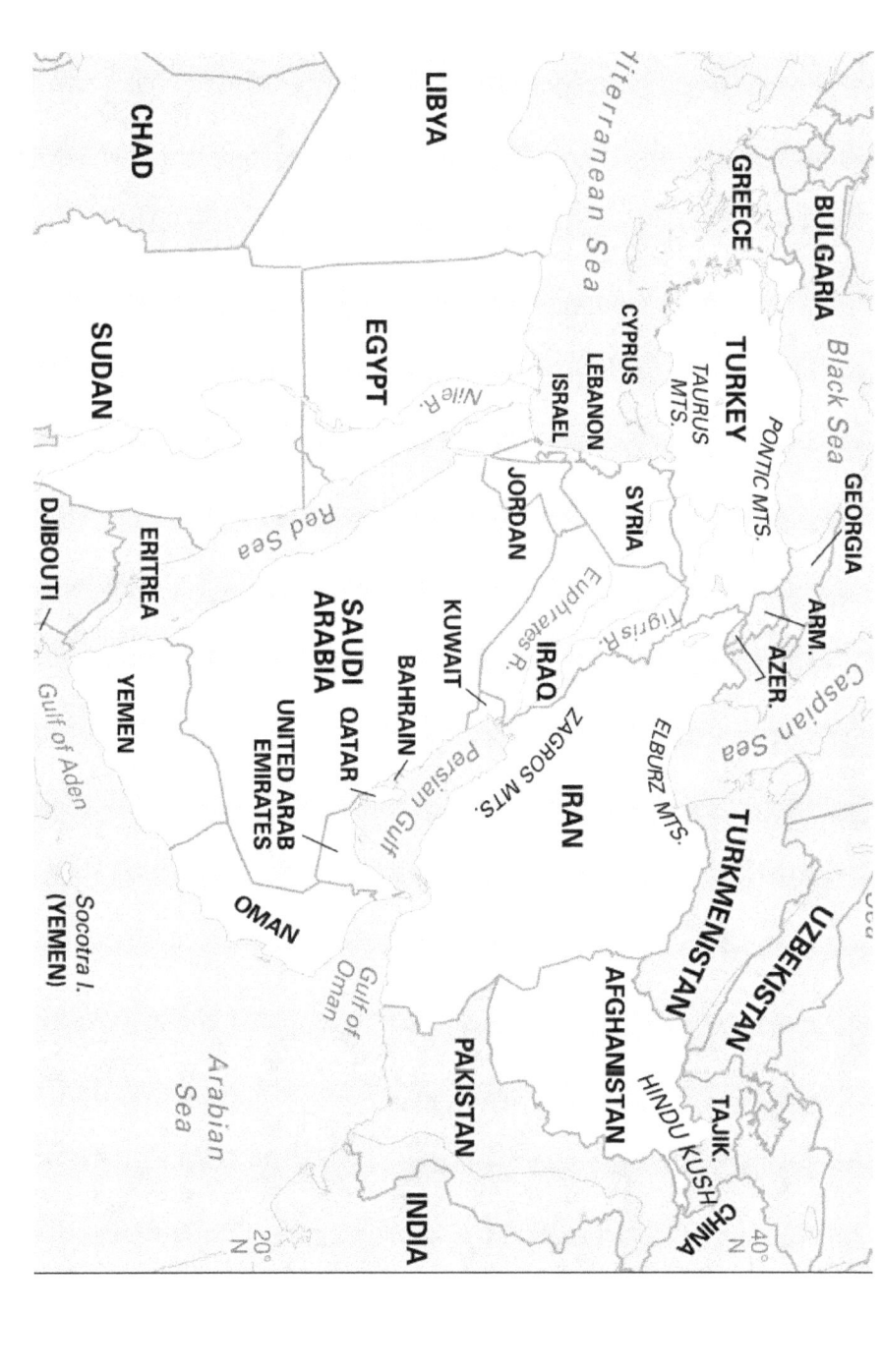

Foreword

I have known Lara Kajs for nearly two decades. We both serve in humanitarian service, and I am pleased to see her return to the place where our journey began… Syria.

Lara is one of the most compassionate, brilliant, and dedicated people I have ever met, and she is also one of the most courageous. She would not think twice about running into the fire and is not afraid to get into the mix. In fact, when the crisis began in Syria, she managed to put together sources, joined a humanitarian effort with boots on the ground, and went to Damascus to see it for herself.

She is seldom part of any compromise, and the uniqueness of her life, lifestyle, extended family dynamics, and leadership reflects the conscious choices she made to do things differently… to march to the beat of the music she chooses.

Her honesty can sometimes be "in your face", but that is part of what I love and respect about her; you never have to wonder what Lara is thinking. If you do not know, you are not listening. I never have to guess what she thinks about a situation – because it comes across loud and clear in her writing, whether it is for TGR or commentary on her blog, Thinking Out Loud, or in one of her books. Her words are her commitment to the situation. If she does not know something, she will not make it up, but straight-up say she does not know… and then go find out the answer. In a world of ambiguity and double-talk, it is refreshing to see someone not afraid to call it out.

We have shared a lot of meals, traveled the world together, and yes, even dodged some bombs and bullets. I have watched her weather many storms, bask in the sunlight, relish in the good times, and hunker down in the bad.

She is the founder and executive director of the NGO nonprofit, The Genocide Report – and Feast or Famine – she is committed to the work. The human part that is ingrained in her DNA… to serve.

Lara changed my life and perspective in so many ways, for the better, and her words can change yours if you keep an open heart and open mind.

So pay attention… as Lara's mom likes to joke – you are about to get a very human history lesson.

Warm Regards,

Dr. Jason Nzari

Rafah, Gaza, December 2024

Preface

My introduction to atrocities began as an undergrad at the University of Hawai'i in 1999 and continued through three graduate degrees. So, I have been studying and working in this field for over twenty-five years., and I have witnessed firsthand the atrocities and human suffering I speak of and write about. In some respects, I have seen more of the devastation of war than most military service members, and it never gets any easier to see what happens when corrupt leaders become more interested in themselves than in serving their country or its people. I found this to be the case, especially concerning Bashar al-Assad in Syria.

I am the founder and executive director of The Genocide Report (TGR) an NGO nonprofit in Washington, DC. I started TGR in November 2011 because of Assad's brutal attacks on his people following the peaceful protests of the Arab Spring, and the unprecedented displacement and humanitarian crisis that ensued.

After thirty years of government corruption, suppressed freedoms, and economic repression under Hafez al-Assad, those issues were further exacerbated by twenty-four more years under his son, Bashar. For more than five decades, the Assad family brutalized the Syrian people.

While the Arab Spring created an opportunity for the people to express their concerns, their cries fell on deaf ears. As demonstrations increased and calls for Assad's resignation grew louder, the regime ordered the military to use deadly force to crush the protestors, resulting in open conflict.

At least 600,000 people were killed, but that number is likely much higher. The war forcibly displaced more than half of Syria's pre-war population of twenty-two million. Seven million were permanently internally displaced. Türkiye, Jordan, and Lebanon host nearly eighty-four percent of the people forced to flee, crossing borders. The UN reports that 16.7 million people in Syria need some form of humanitarian assistance with as many as five million in critical need. At least a half million children are chronically malnourished.

The amount of human suffering in Syria was compounded by more than a decade of forced displacement, indiscriminate attacks on civilians, chlorine barrel bombs, sarin gas attacks, forced disappearances, besiegement, starvation, torture, sexual assault, extrajudicial killings, unlawful imprisonment, and mass executions. All of this lies at the feet of Bashar al-Assad.

Assad had an opportunity to be a reformer – but he chose to destroy his country... his people, instead.

Although some may compare the Syrian conflict to others, in truth, it cannot compare to any other. It is worse because it started as a peaceful protest. The people wanted a voice in government, a say in leadership, freedom, and a chance for a true democracy, and not a dictatorship. And they were crushed by government violence.

How bad does it have to be before you pack your family up, taking with you only what you can carry, and flee your home country… knowing that nothing is certain? How bad does it have to be, when you are willing to risk your life, and the lives of your family members to seek safety? These questions do not apply only to Syria. The same questions can be applied to every single person who is forced to flee what they know and cross a border into the unknown with the hope that they will be safe and find peace.

War is the quiet bravery of civilians who will endure far more than I ever will. Those expected to fight and those just trying to survive. Mothers, fathers, sons, and daughters are forever and indelibly traumatized by the horrors forced upon them… grieving and in despair. These are their stories.

Acknowledgments

There is no question who deserves my deepest gratitude… the people of Syria… who trusted me with their stories. Every source who provided me with information kept me updated on the situation on the ground and shared their trauma with me, I am profoundly grateful. From my first trip in 2012 to my last in 2021, the kindness you showed me – even in your darkest moments, will never be forgotten. To those who could not go on the record – Thank You – for the countless hours you spent with me, helping me to understand more clearly all that needed to get out. I'm in your debt.

The world is better with humanitarians who share their love for humanity and passion for serving. What we do is a collaborative effort. Without those collaborative efforts, nothing would ever get done. And so I am grateful for the shared efforts of the Syrian Emergency Task Force and the Syrian Civil Defense (The White Helmets - who came to my rescue more than once), the Syria Justice and Accountability Center, the International Commission on Missing Persons, the UN Independent Institution on Mission Persons, ICRC, MSF, Witness, Genocide Watch,

Human Rights Watch, Amnesty International, IRC, the UN, and The Genocide Report.

I'm deeply grateful for the work of Yakzan Shishakly and Maram Foundation for the incredible work they have done over the past thirteen years, taking care of the people… especially women and children. New beginnings are often fraught with a period of cleaning up the old. Stay strong my friends… a new Syria is on the horizon.

My sincerest appreciation goes to Craig, whose guidance, coaching, and expertise were instrumental in shaping the direction of my career.

My heartfelt thanks to Alex who saw the potential in me before I did. Your encouragement never fails.

My deepest gratitude to Jason for his unwavering support throughout this journey, and whose late-night talks made all the difference.

Special thanks to Chad for believing in this work – and so many others - and championing it tirelessly, enduring late nights and countless revisions with a smile and lots of advice.

Stephanie and Noelle deserve a round of applause for their insightful feedback and dedication to shaping this book. Many thanks!

To Brad's mom, Elizabeth, who has experienced something no parent should have to face – on many levels. Thank you for sharing Brad with us. He is loved, he is missed, and he will never be forgotten.

My heartfelt thanks to Karen Whited Haun whose encouragement and support never fails, and always lifts. You have been my bestie for more than a minute. Thanks for everything!

To the readers, students, and faculty members, who embark on this journey of discovery and understanding with me. I appreciate the attention and hope that you walk away with a lot of questions and the desire to demand the answers.

To the many peaceful protesters around the world who join arms, lift their voices, and call for change, your bravery is inspiring!

To the scholars who paved the way in the field of atrocity studies and human rights, your groundbreaking work laid the foundation for this exploration. Although there are times when even I wonder how I ended up on this path… I am grateful to be on it.

For my mom: "But those who hope in the Lord will renew their strength, They will soar on wings like eagles; they will run and not grow weary, they will walk and not faint." ~ Isaiah 40:31. Mom, your support, love, and advice are immeasurable… and I am so grateful.

My deepest gratitude to CFKW ~ How is it that my "moment" turns around when I hear your voice? I guess you just have that effect. Seriously… you could be singing the alphabet backward… and although it might not make sense… it would still heal the soul. And so you are still "there in spirit" and I am grateful.

Without the experiences and support from my peers and "dream team" at TGR, this book would not exist. You have allowed me to lead a great group of humanitarians, and to be a leader of amazing leaders is a blessing. Thank you to Chad, Alex, Jason, Noelle, and Stephanie.

With gratitude,

Lara Kajs

Washington, DC, February 2025

larakajs@thegenocidereport.org

Chapter One
Al Assad

Dictators enjoy holding onto power, and sometimes longevity is a family affair. The al-Assad family ruled Syria for fifty-four years. The father, Hafez, seized power in 1970, and then the power was willed to his son, Bashar, in 2000.

The family motto for what was best for the country was that they either stayed in power or burned it to the ground. And that is, more or less, what they did. This "burn it down" mentality was how they dealt with their people and the outside world as well.

The Assad regime was a highly personalist dictatorship, which governed Syria as a totalitarian police state, and was marked by severe repression, numerous human rights violations, and war crimes.

Outlasting ten American presidents, the regime managed to retain its iron grip while regional countries went through massive upheavals, culminating in the establishment of new leaders, and the removal of old ones. But the Assad family remained.

The Rise of Hafez al-Assad

The father, Hafez al-Assad, was born into an impoverished family of Alawite heritage. He rose through the Ba'ath Party ranks to take control of the Syrian branch of the party in the Corrective Movement1, resulting in his rise to the Syrian presidency. But Syria's history has been chaotic and violent.

In the aftermath of gaining independence, most Arab countries experienced extreme political instability. Many states struggled to traverse a period that was defined by dynamic ideological interests. The most prominent of which was Arab nationalism.2 Intense efforts from nationalists following WWII secured Syrian independence in 1946. However, Syrians would discover that war would be a thorn in its side during its nation-building mission.

The establishment of the state of Israel in 19483, further complicated relations between the Arab and Muslim world and its new neighbors. The Syrian military was inexperienced and inefficient, and consequently defeated in northern Palestine and was forced to sign a ceasefire with Israel in 1949. That year proved to be pivotal for modern Syrian history because before the war was even over, the country had the first of its many coups.

In March 1949, Army Chief of Staff Husni al-Zaim used political instability and military humiliation at the hands of Israel, as justification for his bloodless military coup. Within the context of the Cold War, President Shukri al-Quwatli had allowed a strong communist party presence within his country. In the years following al-Zaim's coup, there were allegations of US involvement. The domino effect had begun.

Before the end of the year, Adib al-Shishakly completed another series of rebellions. Even though the Syrian economy grew substantially during the 1950s, political instability continued. To solidify his control, al-Shishakly violently repressed the Druze, a more independent-minded group in the country. His desire to build a totalitarian regime upset the influential political and merchant classes. As a result, in 1954, another coup took place, which had the support of a wide base across the political scene.

Rife with tension, the prominence of the left, drew the country into the rivalry between the United States and the USSR. However, while Syria was experiencing extreme instability, Egypt had been propelled into a regional leadership role thanks to the modernization it experienced under a Pan-Arab socialist government that had inspired the Arab world. Jamal al Nasser's message of Arab unity made him wildly popular, especially in Syria.

In February 1958, Syria gave up its sovereignty by unifying with Egypt, becoming the "Northern Province" and forming the United Arab Republic (UAR) which was led by Nasser. However, the euphoria of the merger subsided when it became clear that Egypt would dominate Syria.

Governmental positions of importance in Syria were filled by Egyptians. Nasser dealt with Syria's political instability by banning all political parties including the overwhelmingly popular Ba'ath party. At the UAR's direction, Syria's economy took on a socialist orientation, something that did not set well with the majority of merchant families that dominated Syrian society The attitude was that Egypt was acting like it owned Syria.

In 1961, disgruntled Syrian officers staged a coup. At the end of it, the UAR was broken up and Syria was once again a sovereign country. However, independence did not miraculously grant stability. Over the next eighteen months, the country would experience a wave of rebellions.

In March 1963, Ba'ath military officers launched an insurrection for a power grab. A month before, the Iraqi Ba'ath party also took power by force. Ba'athism, from the Arabic word Ba'ath meaning resurrection, was an ideology that promoted Pan-Arab anti-imperialist and Arab socialist ideals. The Ba'ath party in Syria was split between the military committee led by Salah Jadid and Hafez al-Assad, and the civilian faction led by its ideological founders Michel Aflaq and Salah al-din al-Bitar.

An internal struggle developed within the Ba'ath party between the old guard led by Aflaq and al-Bitar versus the radical new guard represented by Jadid and al-Assad. In the 1966 coup, led by Salah Jadid (Alawite), Salun Hatan (Druze), Hafez al-Assad (Alawite), and Mustafa

Tlass (Sunni), the new guard emerged victorious and subsequently hijacked the leadership of the Ba'ath party in Syria.

The Ba'athist power grab sealed Syria's fate as it provided the nail in the coffin for any chance for democracy. The ability to dissent was banned. There was also a shift in who monopolized power as the country's Sunni majority lost control. The new government pursued socialist policies which challenged the prominence of established political and merchant families.

In 1967, Syria was attacked by Israel during the 6-Day War4. In the aftermath of the war, Israel began an illegal occupation of the strategically important Golan Heights and forced 100,000 people to flee as refugees. The Ba'athist governing council was once again immersed in internal conflict between Jadid and al-Assad, the latter assuming power.

Syria, a key center of Pan-Arab ideas represented the political instability of the period having to contend with an aggressive new neighbor in Israel and the rise of an increasingly assertive Ba'ath Party. The country went through countless changes in government until power was centralized in the hands of Hafez al-Assad in 1970.

Hafez was an old-school style of dictator. There are accounts that he ordered soldiers to kill puppies, and female soldiers were forced to bite off the heads of snakes. He promoted his supporters within the Ba'ath Party, many of whom were also of Alawite heritage. After the revolution,

Alawite strongmen were installed while Druze and Sunnis were removed from the army and the Ba'ath Party.

Hafez al-Assad's thirty years of military rule witnessed the transformation of Syria into a dynastic dictatorship. The new political system was led by the Ba'ath Party elites dominated by the Alawites, who were intensely loyal to the Assad family and controlled the military, security forces, and secret police.

When he launched his Corrective Revolution in 1970, Hafez al-Assad mixed his strategic intelligence with unprecedented brutality to ensure he did not one day suffer the same fate as his predecessors. To do this he cemented his rule by capitalizing on Syria's religious diversity and divisions, while at the same time, promoting the idea of Syria being one Arab nation with an eternal message.

He stacked the Syrian political chambers with Sunnis to satisfy a potentially hostile majority, while the armed forces were over-represented by his fellow Alawites. Similarly, to appeal to upper society, he allowed for some economic freedoms and relaxed some of the reforms of the sixties. The fact that the country was being run by an Alawite proved to be a controversial issue especially since the Alawites are an offshoot of Shia Islam and considered heretical by some of the country's majority Sunnis.

Even though he tried to portray himself as a devout Muslim al-Assad alienated many with the secular nature of his 1973 constitution. Perhaps the biggest challenge to his authority came from the Islamist groups, who launched an uprising in 1976, that lasted six years and thrust the Muslim Brotherhood into insurrection leadership. Hafez al-Assad crushed the uprising in the 1982 Hama Massacre during which his security forces killed tens of thousands of citizens. It was termed the single deadliest act by any Arab government against its people in the modern Middle East. The three-week massacre resulted in the Syrian regime's crackdown on insurgents and innocent civilians of Hama.

Foreign policy-wise, al-Assad was largely preoccupied with two issues: Israel, to whom it had already suffered loss, and its other neighbor, Lebanon, for whom it had intervened during the Lebanese civil war. The Syrian intervention in Lebanon would go on to draw international criticism for its domination of the country.

Hafez al-Assad was the master of the "Hamburger Trick". Which is to say a trick that involves an act of diplomatic sleight of hand. In theory, the customer takes the bread, which has a bit of meat sticking out at the edges, and the seller withdraws the hamburger. The trick is to get someone to believe they are buying something they want, but in the end, when it is too late, they are fooled. Meanwhile, the seller has the money. And that was the whole sum of how the regime operated. Everything was for his benefit.

In December 1999, the Clinton Administration hosted a series of peace talks between Syria and Israel, ending in a stalemate in the talks.

Within the context of this period, the administration thought that Hafez Al-Assad would foster a partnership through Syria that would lead to comprehensive Arab-Israel peace. At least that is how it was framed at the time. However, Hafez sent a message to the Americans that chiefly stated let me take care of my power. I will engage in peace talks but don't interfere in what I'm doing domestically, and the Clinton administration more or less went along with that.

Hafez resurrected the Ba'ath Party in Syria and built up its military with the help of the Soviets. When he died in 2000 his son Bashar, the British-trained ophthalmologist took over. Bashar was seen as a potential reformer right up until March 2011, when pro-democracy demonstrations were met with brutal government force.

Bashar: Like Father, Like Son

Hafez al-Assad and his wife, Anissa, had six children: four sons and two daughters. Three of their children are deceased: a daughter named Bushra who died in infancy, a son named Majd who died in 2009 after a long illness, and Bassel, the heir apparent who was killed in a car accident in 1994. The living children: a second daughter, also named Bushra, a son named Maher who led the military police, and Bashar, an ophthalmologist who became the heir apparent after the death of Bassel, and the dictator after their father died.

Shortly after Bassel died in a car accident in 1994, Bashar was recalled from London, by the Syrian Army. He became the heir apparent, and over the next six years, Hafez prepared Bashar for his succession.

General Bahjat Suleiman, in the Defense Companies, was assigned to oversee Bashar's preparation for a smooth transition. These objectives were addressed on three levels: support for Bashar in the military and security apparatus; Bashar's public image; and training in the mechanisms of running the country.

To establish his credentials in the military, Bashar entered the military academy in Homs in 1994. He was propelled through the ranks to become a colonel of the Syrian Republican Guard in January 1999. To form a military power base for Bashar, old divisional commanders in his father's service, were pushed into retirement, and new young, Alawite officers with loyalties to him took their place.

In 1998, Bashar took charge of Syria's Lebanon file, which had been handled, since the 70s, by Vice President Abdul Halim Khaddam, who had been a potential contender for president. By taking charge of Syrian affairs in Lebanon, Bashar was able to push Khaddam aside and establish a new power base in Lebanon.

In the same year, Bashar installed Emile Lahoud, a loyal Assad ally, as the President of Lebanon. The act pushed former Lebanese Prime Minster Rafic Hariri aside and from consideration as Prime Minister. To further weaken the old Syrian order in Lebanon, Bashar replaced Ghazi

Kanaan, the long-serving de facto Syrian High Commissioner in Lebanon, with Rustum Ghazaleh.

Similarly to his military career, Bashar was engaged in public affairs. He was given expansive powers and commissioned to head the bureau which received complaints and appeals from citizens. He led a campaign against corruption which resulted in many of his potential rivals for president being put on trial for corruption. Bashar also became the President of the Syrian Computer Society and helped to introduce the internet to Syria, which elevated his image as a modernizer and reformer. The Ba'athist party, military, and the Alawite sect were supportive of Bashar al-Assad enabling him to become his father's successor.

After the death of Hafez al-Assad on 10 June 2000, the Constitution of Syria was amended. The minimum age requirement for the presidency was lowered from 40 to 34, which was Bashar's age at the time. The sole candidate of the presidential referendum, Assad was subsequently confirmed president on 10 July 2000, with 97.29 percent support for his leadership. In line with his role as President of Syria, he was also appointed the commander-in-chief of the Syrian Armed Forces and Regional Secretary-General of the Central Command of the Arab Socialist Ba'ath Party.

At the funeral of Hafez Al-Assad in 2000, Madeline Albright was sent on behalf of the United States. There is a moment when she meets Bashar Al-Assad briefly, and then she comes out and makes a statement to the media that she is comforted by the fact that he is going to take the same path as his father. The regime insiders, the Tlass family, and the primary components all breathed a sigh of relief. But the reality was that the hope of the world, and especially the hope of the people, was that Bashar would be a different leader for Syria and not the same.

Immediately after he took office, Bashar implemented a series of crackdowns in 2000-01. A reform movement known as the Damascus Spring5 led by writers, intellectuals, dissidents, cultural activists, and others, was marked by calls for transparency and democracy and the end of the state of emergency established by his father. The movement led to the closing of Mezzeh Prison, the declaration of a wide-ranging amnesty, and the release of hundreds of Muslim Brotherhood-affiliated political prisoners. However, security crackdowns were launched again within the year. Hundreds of intellectuals were arrested, targeted, exiled, or sent to prison and the state of emergency was continued. The early concessions were rolled back to tighten authoritarian control, censorship was increased, and the Damascus Spring movement was banned in the interest of national unity and stability.

The regime's policy of a "social market economy" became a symbol of corruption, as Assad's loyalists became its sole beneficiaries. Several discussion forums were shut down and many intellectuals were abducted by the Mukhabarat, tortured, and killed. Many analysts believe that the initial promises of opening up were part of a government strategy to find Syrians who were not supportive of the new leadership.

While the Assad government described itself as secular, various political scientists and observers noted that his regime exploited sectarian tensions in the country. Although Assad inherited power structures and a cult of personality nurtured by his father, he lacked the loyalty received by his father and faced rising discontent against his rule. As a result, many people from his father's regime resigned or were purged, and the political inner circle was replaced by staunch loyalists from Alawite clans. Assads early economic liberalization programs worsened inequalities and centralized the socio-political power of the loyalist Damascus elite of the Assad family, alienating the Syrian rural population, urban working classes, businessmen, industrialists, and people from one-traditional Ba'ath strongholds.

Although he publicly condemned the US invasion of Afghanistan, and privately, he criticized the September 11th attacks. Syria emerged as one of the CIA's most effective intelligence allies in the fight against al-Qaeda. Syria closely cooperated with the agency's detention and interrogation programs, including the extraordinary rendition program, of people deemed as enemy combatants. Syrian prisons were a major site of "rendition"6 where prisoners were tortured by Syrian interrogators on behalf of the agency.

But Bashar was playing both sides. After the start of the US-Iraq War in 2003, he secretly released Islamist fighters from prison and sent them over the border into Iraq to fight the Americans. Donald Rumsfeld announced that the Syrian government was arming the Islamist fighters. Of course, a few years later, the same fighters would sneak back into Syria and establish the Islamic State.

Syria had long had its hands in control in Lebanon, but in 2004, Rafic Hariri, the former Prime Minister wanted Syria out of Lebanon, and the UN sided with Lebanon and told Syria to get out of the country. But controlling Lebanon was one of Hafez's greatest achievements, and Bashar had a choice to either get out of Lebanon or to ignore the United Nations. He chose the latter.

On 14 February 2005, Rafic Hariri was assassinated in a massive truck bomb explosion in Beirut, killing twenty-two people. Syria was widely blamed for Hariri's murder. In the months leading to the assassination, relations between Hariri and Bashar plunged amid a tone of threats and intimidation. Bashar promoted his brother-in-law Assef Shawkat, a key figure suspected of orchestrating the terrorist attack, as the chief of the Syrian Military Intelligence Directorate immediately after Hariri's death.

The UN launched an investigation, but the investigation was sidetracked. The bomber suspect in the assassination gave testimony to investigators and then committed suicide. Star witness recanted their testimonies. The son of the UN investigator was killed, and in fear for his life, he quit. The killings triggered an intifada in Lebanon as hundreds of thousands of protesters poured into the streets to demand a total withdrawal of Syrian military forces.

Mounting international pressure called on Syria to implement the UN Security Council Resolution 15597. On 5 March 2005, Assad ordered the departure of Syrian soldiers and by 5 May, the UN officially confirmed the total departure of all Syrian soldiers, ending the twenty-nine-year military occupation. The uprisings became known as The Cedar Revolution.

The UN investigation commission report published on 20 October 2005 revealed that high-ranking members of Syrian intelligence and the Assad family had directly supervised the killing, although Assad strongly denied it. On 27 May 2007 Assad was approved for another seven-year term with 97.6 percent of the votes supporting his continued leadership. Opposition parties were not allowed in the country, and Assad was the only candidate in the referendum. In 2007, Bashar al-Assad implemented numerous measures that further intensified political and cultural repression in Syria. Travel bans were expanded against dissidents, intellectuals, authors, and artists living in Syria, preventing them and their families from traveling abroad.

The Winds of Protest and Reform

In 2010, the Syrian government was described as the worst offender among Arab states for its restriction of free movement. Bashar al-Assad was responsible for one of the most repressive regimes in modern history. Assad's first decade in power was marked by extensive censorship, summary executions, forced disappearance, discrimination of ethnic minorities, and extensive surveillance by the Ba'athist secret police.

But in 2011, the winds of protest and reform from North Africa shifted. After blowing through Tunisia, then Libya, Egypt, and Yemen, the winds turned to Syria. This was the fork in the road moment for Assad; to give the people the reforms they wanted and bring about peace in his country, or to use violence and crackdowns to subject them to more of the same. He determined that protest and reform would not happen in Syria.

The Syrian civil war began on 15 March 2011. And it continued until the fall of Bashar al-Assad on Sunday, 8 December 2024. A ruthless totalitarian dictator – a strongman – as that term has been tossed about lately. But his "strongman" identity is false because it was not earned by defending his people, but by bullying them, and terrorizing them.

A strong man does not use Sarin gas on children. A strong man does not drop chlorine barrel bombs on civilians. A strong man does not torture, mass execute, or order rape to disgrace females and tear families apart. Those are not qualities of a strong man… they are not qualities of a man at all. But they are the characteristics of a dictator terrorist.

The peaceful protests came on the backs of all of the Arab Spring uprisings. On one hand, Syria and the House of Assad had been through this before. But on the other hand, this time was different. The Assad family watched as other regimes had been toppled by the people. Now they have protest marches in Syria. And so Bashar al-Assad made the conscious decision that Syria would not end up like Tunisia, Libya, or Egypt.

Immediately, Maher, who led the 4th Division, an elite division of the army, and a cousin, Hafez Makhlouf, who served as an intelligence chief, gave the orders to "shoot to kill" unarmed demonstrators, to scare people off the streets, and that is exactly what happened.

Every attempt by the protestors in Damascus, and in other major cities like Homs, and Daraa, to occupy a square because they looked to Egypt as the example to follow. They wanted a Tahir Square moment, like in Cairo, where they could protest, and the world would watch, and change would come. And every attempt by peaceful Syrians was extinguished with bullets and blood.

During an attempt for peaceful demonstrations in Damascus, the Syrian military opened fire on unarmed civilians who were just trying to occupy a square. The same thing happened in Homs. The orders were coming from Assad.

In Hama, during a large, peaceful demonstration in June 2011, protesters managed to occupy a square on the day the US and French ambassadors visited. The protesters thought that maybe the dignitaries would provide them some protection. But the military surrounded the demonstration and opened fire on the square, and hundreds were killed.

During the Obama administration, the international community watched and waited for what it thought would be the end of the Assad family's hold on Syria. Obama came out and said Bashar al-Assad had to leave, he must go. Of course that didn't happen. The US, the European Union, and the majority of the Arab League called for Assad to resign in 2011, but he refused, and the war continued.

Syria was not a US priority – not in the same way that Russia, Iran, and Türkiye saw it. After wars in Afghanistan and Iraq, which are viewed by most American citizens as failures, nobody prioritized the idea of "Assad must go."

Under Trump, "America First" said no new wars would start. And while he was willing to engage in some isolated bombing to stop the Syrians from attacking their citizens with chemical weapons, after that it was left to Assad.

The least that could have happened was for there to have been a safe zone in northern Syria and Türkiye. A no-fly zone would have been feasible. It would have stemmed the tide of the refugees that were going into Türkiye. The thinking in the Obama administration at the time was that this was a slippery slope toward an Iraq-like intervention. As a consequence, real help did not come, and even the UN, for the most part, went along with that.

A series of state elections were held every seven years which Assad won with an overwhelming majority of votes. In the 2007 election, Bashar was the only person on the ballot. Yet he thought his ninety-seven percent victory indicated the entire country loved and approved of him.

The elections were unanimously regarded by independent observers as a sham process and boycotted by the opposition. The last two elections 2014 and 2021 were conducted only in areas controlled by the Syrian government during the country's ongoing civil war and condemned by the UN.

Having spent some time on the ground and experienced the revolution and the consequences of war, it was surprising to me that the average person watching the media coverage did not understand that the Assads did not care how many people died, how many fled the country, or what happened in the end, except that they had to stay in power. So, squashing the peaceful protests was necessary to maintain the status quo.

Few people know that Hafez faced similar challenges in the late 70s and early 80s. It was not only Islamist insurgents that challenged the power paradigm. When people think of that era they immediately think of the Muslim Brotherhood and its armed wing that challenged the regime, but there was a secular protest movement against the regime in the early 70s. Hafez maintained order, but he did it by exerting absolute authoritarian control.

And like his son, 30 years later, Hafez went after the peaceful protesters first. He wanted to get those people out of the picture first, and all the while, he continued to deny the brutalities. He argued that the order was to implement action and maintain peace, but continued to deny that there was a command to kill.

And like father, like son, Bashar claimed to be fighting a war on terrorism. So, the father taught the son how to maintain a grip on power. That is the most revealing aspect of it.

Even the tactics were similar. But obviously, the devastation under Bashar was 1,000 times more so. Hafez al-Assad's battle culminated in one massacre in the town of Hama, where tens of thousands were killed. Whereas Bashar al-Assad essentially had a Hama in every neighborhood, in every town, in every governorate in the country, that stood against the regime. When Hafez died and power was transferred to Bashar, with no military background,.. a physician - eye doctor - certainly the hope was that he would be more oriented toward the West, and perhaps a more compassionate leader.

Bashar ended up assuming the power, but he didn't have to work for it, the father did. Hafez al-Assad and Mustafa Tlass built the regime, but Bashar inherited it. What could have been a lasting legacy, turned into the worst humanitarian disaster… ever.

Notes

[1] The Corrective Movement, also known as the Corrective Revolution or the 1970 Coup, was a bloodless military coup led by General Hafez al-Assad on 13 November 1970 – with the promise to sustain and improve the nationalist socialist line of the Ba'ath Party.

[2] Arab Nationalism is a political ideology that promotes the unification of Arab-speaking people into a single nation. It emphasizes Arab culture, history, and language. Arab Nationalism emerged in the 19th century as a response to Western dominance. Based on the idea that Arab States share a common identity. The common goal of Arab Nationalism is to break down the borders between Arab states, create a united state, promote Arab culture and civilization, and celebrate Arab history, language, and literature. Generally speaking, nationalism is an ideology that prioritizes one nation or nationality over others. It emphasizes promoting the culture and interests of the nation.

[3] The UN establishment of Israel 1948 Resolution 181, also known as the Partition Resolution divided Great Britain's former Palestinian mandate into Jewish Arab States in May 1949 when the British mandate was scheduled to end. Resolution 181 was a UN General Assembly decision to split Palestine into Jewish and Arab States in 1947. The resolution was adopted on 29 November 1947 and included the following provisions: 1) The area around Jerusalem which is significantly religious would be under international control administered by the UN, 2) The resolution called for the creation of two independent states, one Arab and one Jewish, and 3) The resolution was drafted by the UN Special Committee on Palestine on 3 September 1947. The resolution was met with acceptance by Jews but rejection by Arabs. Some consider the resolution to be one of the most remarkable in the history of the UN.

[4] Also known as the Yom Kippur War or the Ramadan War. After three wars in 1949, 1956, and 1967, Israel had expanded its territory, leading to increased tensions with the Arab States. On 6 October 1973, an Arab coalition of Egyptian and Syrian forces launched a surprise attack on Israel's Yom Kippur holiday, in an effort to regain lost territory.

[5] The Damascus Spring was a period of intense, political and social debate in Syrian which started after the death of Hafez al-Assad in June 2000 and continued until autumn fo 2001, when most ot the activities associated with it were suppressed by the Bashar al-Assad government.

---

[6] The CIA used Syria as an illicit base of operations for its extraordinary rendition program for the purposes of torturing people the agency labeled as "ghost detainees. Extraordinary Rendition was established in the 1990s, but expanded in the 2000s during the US "War on Terror." Victims of rendition were subjected to physical and psychological torture. Physical torture included beatings on palms, face, back of the neck, hips, and lower back with two inch thick electric cables, fists, placed on spine breaking chair, hanged upside down in a tire, and electric shocks. Psychological torture included being placed in a room and forced to listen to the screens of other being tortured. In Syria, most of the extraordinary renditions were carried out at the Palestine branch prison or Sednaya. One former CIA agent described the policy as if You want a serious interrogation send a prisoner to Jordan… if you want them tortured, send them to Syria… if you want them to disappear, send them to Egypt." Syria was the most common destination for rendered suspects under the CIA program.

[7] United Nations Security Council Resolution 1559 was adopted on 2 September 2004 to address the situation in Lebanon. The resolution called for the withdrawal of foreign forces, the disarming of militias, and the support of free elections. The resolution called for the Lebanese government to have sole control of all Lebanese territory.

Chapter Two
Peaceful Protests to War

Mohamed Bouazizi. His name may not be known to you, but his death led to one of the largest movements in history, that initiated the toppling of three regimes, triggered two brutal decade-long wars, and eventually the collapse of the Assad regime in Syria. The fruit seller of Tunisia started the Arab Spring.

Due to high unemployment, food inflation, government corruption, repressed political freedoms, and poor living conditions, Mohamed Bouazizi had few choices for taking care of his family. Unable to find work, he sold fruit at a stand, in Sidi Bouzid, Tunisia.

On 17 December 2010, a municipal inspector confiscated his fruit, kicked over his cart, and humiliated him publicly. Bouazizi went to the governor's office to file a complaint but was sent away, unable to be heard. In an act of defiance and maybe desperate humiliation and hopelessness, he purchased a can of gasoline and returned to the governor's office. Then, on the street, in the middle of traffic, he poured the gasoline over his body and lit a match.

Bouazizi suffered burns to ninety percent of his body. He lingered in a coma for nineteen days. On 4 January 2011, Mohamed Bouazizi died. His gravestone reads: "Martyr Mohamed Bouazizi. Peace for his life. And in the next life, have peace as well."

In the aftermath of Bouazizi's self-immolation and death, a series of anti-government protests, uprisings, and armed rebellions spread throughout the Middle East and Northern Africa (MENA). The first to fall was Tunisia. From Tunisia, the protests spread to five other countries, Libya, Egypt, Bahrain, Yemen, and Syria. Thus began the Arab Spring.

Dissatisfaction with economic decline, overwhelming unemployment, needed reforms, political corruption, extreme poverty, and human rights violations, became the catalyst for the Arab Spring. Protests against lack of transparency, oversight, and accountability, especially the concentration of wealth (and its redistribution) in the hands of dictators who had held power for decades, and the refusal of the youth and unions to accept the status quo, took shape and began to push for change. What was happening was a young generation peacefully rising against oppressive regimes, to secure a more democratic political system and more promising economic possibilities.

Recognizing that digital technologies have immense power to support united action, such as the demand for political and social change, protesters turned to social media as a means for collective activism and to bypass state-operated media channels. Except in Libya, the use of social media platforms more than doubled in Arab countries during the Arab Spring protests. The number of Facebook users in the Arab world surpassed 27.7 million people.

While the leadership in some countries changed and regimes were held accountable, in other countries, power vacuums opened across the Arab world. Ultimately, it resulted in a contentious battle between an alliance of power by religious elites and the growing demand for democracy.

The protests led to insurgency in Iraq, the rise of the Islamic State (ISIS/ISIL), and the war that followed. The world witnessed the fall and execution of Muammar Gaddafi and the insurgency that followed as ISIS seized power. In Egypt, there was the fall of Hosni Mubarak, the election and removal of Mohamed Morsi, and the installation of el-Sisi. Protests pre-empted the crisis in Yemen as leadership was removed and the Houthi and other sects still compete for power as that civil war continues. And then there is Syria.

Syria was long considered the most restrictive police state in the Arab World, limiting the movement of civilians and other unauthorized individuals within its borders. With tight regulations on independent journalists, the country was listed as one of the worst countries for press freedoms in 2010.

Until the Arab Spring came to Syria, it is important to recall that the last resistance to authoritarian rule was in 1982 with the Hama Massacre under Hafez al-Assad, during which more than 40,000 civilians were killed. Since 1982, Syria has been seemingly calm. But the calm was an illusion. Fear of the Mukhabarat1, the Syrian secret police, was the driving force to the "calm". The Arab Spring gave the people the bravery they needed to demand Bashar al-Assad to resign. As Syrians watched regimes fall in Tunisia, Libya, and Egypt, they saw the same hopeful possibility for Syria.

But Assad was watching what was happening in the region, and even before the uprisings came to Syria, the regime started arresting political dissidents and human rights activists. Many of those arrested were labeled as terrorists. Government forces used Ba'ath party buildings as a base to organize the security forces and to fire on civilians.

However, with all the legitimate reasons to rally and protest, in the city of Daraa, also known as the "Cradle of the Syrian Revolution"2 it was the detention, torture, and death of children that pushed Syrians over the edge and incited revolution.

On 27 February 2011, fourteen-year-old Mouswiya Syasneh, along with a group of teenagers from al-Arbaeem Primary School in Daraa wrote some protest graffiti on a school wall. The messages on the wall read, "Your turn has come, O Doctor" and "The people want the fall of the regime", which became the battle cry of the revolution.

Atef Najib was the head of security in Daraa, he was also a member of the Assad family. For twenty-six days, Najib had the group detained, beaten, and tortured by the Mukhabarat. Najib's actions sparked outrage and led to street demonstrations. He further incited the demonstrators by telling them to "bring their wives to him so he could impregnate them so they could have better children."

Groups began to organize; the people came together. The protests in Daraa on 15 March 2011, began as peaceful, with demonstrators carrying olive branches, unbuttoning their shirts to show they had no weapons, and chanting "peaceful, peaceful." The regime deployed the Syrian Army to quash the uprisings. Soldiers fired on demonstrators.

In the days following the initial protests in Daraa, uprisings continued throughout the country. Across the region, Friday, 18 March became known as the "Friday of Dignity". In Syria, large-scale protests erupted in Daraa, Hama, Deir al-Zor, Damascus, Al-Hasakah, and Baniyas. Police responded with tear gas, water cannons, and beatings.

On 20 March a crowd burned down the Ba'ath Party headquarters and other public buildings. Security Forces responded, firing live ammunition at crowds, and attacking the center of the demonstrations. The two-day assault resulted in the deaths of fifteen civilians and seven police officers. Tens of thousands participated in nationwide mass funeral demonstrations to honor the civilians killed. The demonstrations spread to Hama, Homs, Baniyas, Jasim, Aleppo, Damascus, and Latakia.

Assad blamed the unrest on conspiracies and accused the Syrian opposition of sedition. The government issued an official policy of shoot-to-kill. Security officers who disagreed or held back were fired upon from behind by paramilitaries and the Shabiha death squads. The Shabiha began as an unsavory group, mostly smugglers and racketeers, but evolved to become ultra-loyal enforcers of Syria's brutal regime.

In his first public response to the protests on 30 March 2011, Assad claimed the state was the victim of an international plot. He also criticized the Arab Spring movement and described those participating in the protests as "germs". Assad used medical terminology to describe the different facets of his manner of rule. Assad said, "Germs exist everywhere, on the skin and within the guts. Throughout the history of scientific development, scientists always thought of ways to strengthen the immunity of our bodies. This is what we must think of because it is certainly more important than analyzing the conspiracy."

His analogy of irradicating germs in the body and society has a familiar ring to it. It is not even original. The meaning, of course, is that you can kill tens of thousands of Syrians because they are germs that must be eradicated from society and in the end strengthen Syria. Hitler said the same thing.

Hamza Ali al-Khateeb was a generous boy, and at thirteen years of age, he understood gratitude and compassion. He would ask his parents for money and then give it to the less fortunate. He once asked his father for 100 Syrian pounds, which is about $2. His father said it was too much, but Hamza said, "I have a bed and food while that guy has nothing."

On 29 April 2011, Hamza attended a peaceful demonstration with his family in the village of al-Jeezah in Daraa governorate. As the group walked along the road, military forces fired on them. Hamza was grabbed and detained by Air Force Intelligence.

Almost a month later, on 21 May, Hamza's body was returned to his parents. He had been severely beaten, had multiple broken bones including his jaw and both kneecaps, several gunshot wounds, cigarette burns, electric shock marks, and his genitals had been removed. The autopsy revealed his genitals were removed before he was shot dead. The condition of the body seemed to be a message to the Syrian people about what happens to protestors.

The parents made a video and photos of their son and distributed them to the public and media. The images caused widespread outrage – online, around the world, and among protesters. If Fridays were a day of dignity, then Saturdays became the day of Hamza.

Again, the regime took the position that it was outside international propaganda trying to smear the Assad family. Bashar insisted that no children were being tortured in Syria. When asked about the condition of the body, he said the boy had been dead for over a month and the body was rotting. When asked who killed Hamza, Assad said, "We did."

Hamza had an older brother, Omar, who was arrested in 2018 for refusing to fulfill obligatory military service. He was sent to Sednaya where he died in police custody.

Despite Assad's attempts to crush the protests with suppression and control, mass demonstrations evolved into conflict by the end of April, with pockets of fighting erupting throughout the country. The regime deployed its ground troops and air force, ordering them to fight the protesters and opposition. The international community condemned Assad's deployment of large-scale violence against civilians.

The earliest stages of the opposition (rebel forces) were supported by grassroots organizations that formed during protests. The rebel forces were composed of defected soldiers, from the Syrian Army, and civilian volunteers. Opposition forces began to form across the country and gradually transformed the demonstrations from a civil uprising to an armed rebellion, and later a full-scale civil war. The Free Syrian Army was formed on 29 July 2011 marking the beginning of armed insurrection.

The United States imposed limited sanctions against the Assad government in April 2011, followed by Barack Obama's Executive Order 135733, on 18 May 2011, targeting Basher al-Assad specifically, and six other senior officials. On 23 May 2011, the European Union foreign ministers agreed to impose travel bans and asset freezes on Assad and nine other officials. Canada followed suit imposing sanctions on Syria's leaders including Assad, on 24 May 2011.

In response to the sanctions, as well as the mass migrations, growing displacement crisis, and pressure from the international community, on 20 June 2011, Assad promised a national dialogue that included a movement toward reform, new parliamentary elections, and greater freedoms. He urged refugees to return home from Türkiye while assuring them of amnesty and blaming all unrest on a small number of insurrectionists.

Secretary of State Hillary Clinton stated in July 2011, that Assad had lost legitimacy as president, followed by President Obama's written statement on 18 August 2011, urging Assad to step aside. Neither action managed to persuade Assad but rather made him more intent to retain power, even if it meant civil war for his country.

Not even the UN Security Council could muster the vote. Russia, as a permanent member of the Council, had repeatedly vetoed Western-sponsored draft resolutions that would have left open the possibility of UN sanctions, or maybe military intervention, against the Assad regime.

Opposition forces continued to strengthen from October to December 2011. Protests against the government simultaneously intensified across northern, southern, and western Syria. The uprisings were crushed by massive crackdowns, resulting in tens of thousands of injuries, and hundreds of thousands of deaths. Assad also employed the Shabiha, sectarian death squads, to attack protestors.

The Arab Spring caused the biggest transformation of the Middle East since decolonization. By the beginning of 2012, rulers had been forced from power in Tunisia, Libya, Egypt, and Yemen. But in Syria, Assad proclaimed that "victory was near" and placed the blame for the uprising on foreign countries. The conflict gradually took a more sectarian nature between Sunnis and Shia when the Syrian government began establishing Alawite militias, from Iran, and Hezbollah fighters from Lebanon, to substitute for defected soldiers. A UN report in 2012, described the conflict as "overtly sectarian in nature" although that was denied by both the state and the opposition.

The unprecedented violence and destruction led to a global outcry. The UN Human Rights Council convened an emergency session on 23 April 2012 and tasked a fact-finding mission to investigate the scale of atrocities in Syria. The investigation concluded that the Syrian Army, secret police, and paramilitaries engaged in forced disappearances, massacres, summary executions, sham trials, torture, assassinations, and persecution and abductions of suspects from hospitals, among others, with an official shoot-to-kill policy from the Assad regime.

However, despite aggressive suppression by the state, protest activities by students and youth, and fighting by the armed opposition, continued. Opposition militias captured vast swatches of territory throughout 2012, and by June, both the UN and the International Committee of the Red Cross (ICRC) declared Syria was in a state of civil war.

The wave of initial protests began to fade by mid to late 2012, as many Arab Spring demonstrations were met with violent responses by counter-demonstrators, authorities, pro-government militias, and militaries. In some cases, the attacks were met with violence from protesters.

The TGR team was in the besieged city of Homs in 2012, investigating reported atrocity crimes. Some 28,000 men, women, and children were cold, starving, and defenseless. The electricity had been cut off, there was no communication with the outside world. Families shared what little they had with relatives and neighbors. Civilians were trapped in brutal conditions. Women could not feed their infants. They were giving them sugar and water for weeks.

The Syrian regime claimed it was not targeting civilians, that they were going after terrorists. The team was told not to use cell phones because they could be tracked by the government, and would become a target for missiles and drones. Every single civilian home had been hit in Homs. The top stories of taller buildings were destroyed. Then, the same buildings were repeatedly targeted to cause them to collapse. At that time, there were no military targets in Homs, only civilians trying to stay alive and avoid the conflict.

Syrian Emergency Response counted forty-seven explosions per minute. The explosions began every morning at 6:30 and went into the night. They started with one location and swept the neighborhood with everything they had: mortars, missiles, and snipers.

By early summer, the regime controlled approximately forty percent of the country's territory and sixty percent of the Syrian population. The death toll had surpassed 100,000. Tens of thousands of protesters and fighters had been imprisoned, and there were reports of widespread torture and mass execution.

UNHCR published its report on 18 August 2012 and stated that the atrocities amounted to crimes against humanity with High Commissioner Navi Pillai urging the Security Council members to prosecute Assad in the International Criminal Court. A second emergency session convened by the UNHCR on 22 August 2012 condemned atrocities by the Assad government and called for an immediate ceasefire of all military operations and engagement. Numerous countries demanded Assad's resignation.

Assad maintained that enemies outside of Syria were responsible for the conflict. However, what he did not say was that he had worked out a deal with Iran to send fighters to Syria. Hezbollah entered the war to support the Syrian Army. At the same time, Saudi Arabia and Qatar transferred weapons to the opposition.

International organizations accused both the regime and the opposition of severe human rights violations. In 2013, UN inspections and probes in Syria determined that the Assad regime's abuses were the highest in frequency and scale.

The situation in Syria is partly a consequence of the inability of the UN Security Council to hold perpetrators accountable. Since 2013 the Security Council passed dozens of resolutions on the situation in Syria, however, none of them were fully implemented. The Syrian government deliberately violated most of them. Russia and China tandemly vetoed ten draft resolutions on Syria. Russia independently vetoed eight resolutions systematically shielding Syria from international accountability measures.

A year earlier, in August 2012, President Barack Obama was asked if he would consider using US troops to intervene in Syria. He said that a "red line" was crossed if the Assad regime used chemical weapons in the war. The "red line" he was referring to was the Chemical Weapons Convention, which banned the use of chemical weapons, even during wartime.

Syria's chemical weapons were a major concern during the first few years of the crisis. To some degree, even Russia had questions regarding Syria's chemical weapons. There were profound alarms that these weapons would fall into the hands of terrorists.

In 2013, Syria's chemical weapons capabilities were frightening. With more than 1,200 metric tons stored in at least 23 sites spread across a country about the size of North Dakota, its arsenal of chemical weapons was the third-largest in the world. It was ten times more than the CIA's (defective) 2002 estimate of Iraq's WMD stash and fifty times greater than the arsenal Libya claimed it had in 2011.

But on 21 August 2013, the red line was crossed when the Syrian government used Sarin gas against civilians in the city of Ghouta. Nearly 1,500 civilians including more than 400 children were killed in the gas attack. Horrific video showed people with distorted bodies, stretched out on hospital floors, twitching and foaming at the mouth.

Obama asked Congress for permission to intervene in Syria. However, Congress only allowed "limited and specific" measures against legitimate military targets. But even if all of the measures were met, Congress would not allow US boots on the ground. Congress was not interested in the US intervening in another war in the Middle East.

Although the US and other countries condemned the attacks, no efforts were made to stop the Assad regime from waging chemical warfare against its people. And so Assad took no action as a sign that he could do whatever he wanted, and no one would stop him. Thus, the Syrian people were left to endure the atrocities of the Assad regime.

As the uprisings intensified the Syrian government waged a campaign of arrests that captured tens of thousands of people. In response to the war, Syrian law had been changed to allow police to hold any detained suspect for eight days without a warrant. Arrests focused on two groups: political activists and men and boys from the towns that the Syrian Army had besieged. In the city of al-Rastan in the Homs governorate, more than eighty percent of the population was displaced. Most of the population had been characterized as terrorists.

In February 2014, an agreement called for the evacuation of women, children under the age of fifteen, and elderly men over the age of fifty-five. The deal also called for the delivery of humanitarian aid for those who remained in the city.

Homs was completely besieged and isolated by Assad's forces and had been since the start of the war in 2011. People were starving and had resorted to eating leaves and grass, and whatever else they could find. It had been two years since any humanitarian aid had been allowed into Homs.

The evacuations that day were supposed to be clear-cut and secure. However, immediately, teams came under attack by sniper fire and shelling, despite a planned humanitarian ceasefire. One of those evacuated was an eight-year-old boy named Khaled.

Khaled lived with his father, who lost both his legs at the beginning of the war, his mother, and a sister. Khaled's family had a goat tied up in the back-covered area of their house, about ten yards from the porch. Twice a day Khaled would run to the goat shed to milk it and run back with a pail, trying to avoid Assad's snipers. The day before the evacuation, Khaled had been shot four times. Miraculously, he survived his injuries and was able to receive medical treatment, and his family was evacuated.

Syrians had already witnessed more than 1,000 days of war. On 7 February 2014, there were 130,000 recorded deaths, more than a half-million injured, and six million displaced.

As the conflict escalated, the war shifted from being solely between those for or against the regime. Lines were drawn and outside forces chose sides, armed the opposition, and also armed Assad. Extremist groups such as the Islamic State and Al Qaeda inserted themselves into the war.

By 2015, both Russia and Iran backed Assad, which deepened concern in the international community. Russia used its military bases in Syria for air assaults in support of the Assad regime, frequently targeting civilian communities. Iran deployed thousands of armed Shia Muslim troops, mostly from Lebanon's Hezbollah movement, but also from Afghanistan, Iraq, and Yemen, and spent billions to help Assad.

Opposition forces were supported by Türkiye, the US and UK, France, and other European allies, as well as several Gulf Arab states including Saudi Arabia and Qatar – all eager to counter Iranian influence in the region.

By 2020, a truce negotiated between Russia and Türkiye was designed to bring relief to the region by ending the offensive in northwest Syria. However, the ceasefire was repeatedly violated.

Seven civilians including four children in one family were killed in a Russian airstrike in Idlib in July 2022. Three months later, hostilities increased between Hay'at Tahrir al-Sham (HTS) and other Turkish armed groups, which led to more shelling in Idlib.

In September 2023, hostilities intensified in northwest Syria, with continuous shelling and airstrikes hitting civilian objects and critical infrastructure, including the main power station in the city of Idlib, as well as schools, health facilities displacement camps, markets, and mosques. During their attacks, Syrian forces used incendiary weapons and banned cluster munitions. At least seventy civilians were killed and 303 were injured, while approximately 120,000 people were newly displaced. Hostilities also intensified in the northeast region, displacing tens of thousands of civilians and impacting civilian infrastructure. Attacks by the Islamic State also increased in central Syria, targeting civilians in urban areas.

Since March 2011, the government and opposition groups in Syria have engaged in conflict. The prolonged crisis has its roots in Bashar al-Assad's government's brutal suppression of protests, which quickly devolved into an international and country-wide conflict characterized by rampant atrocity crimes, including the illegal use of chemical weapons.

All the while the Assad regime continued to assert its claim that the conflict that had destroyed the country was a result of "terrorism" conducted by the armed opposition and was sponsored by outside forces. However, the real victims were the innocent civilians who became collateral damage between Assad's forces and the armed opposition. Since 2011, fourteen million people have been forced to flee their homes because of the Syrian war – which makes Syria the world's largest refugee crisis.

In the past two years, the humanitarian crisis in Syria has been compounded by an economic crisis triggered by US sanctions and the Covid pandemic. The country's infrastructure has been decimated by constant shelling and fighting. Syrian currency lost eighty percent of its value and inflation increased to 140 percent at the start of 2022. The poverty rate in Syria is at an unprecedented ninety percent. The war-torn country has been deeply impacted by Covid, resulting in limited testing, a devastated health system, and barely access to vaccines – only 7.4 percent of the population is vaccinated.

UN satellite analysis indicated that more than 35,000 structures were damaged or destroyed in Aleppo alone before 2016. While hospitals are protected under International Humanitarian Law, there have been at least 612 documented attacks on 367 medical facilities, resulting in the deaths of 938 medical personnel. Less than half the country's medical facilities are functional.

The escalation of hostilities that began on 28 November 2024 has impacted citizens, infrastructure, and humanitarian access and operations in a region already strained by prolonged conflict, displacement, and socio-economic collapse.

According to the United Nations, in 2024, at least 1 million people had been newly displaced within Syria, including 155,000 people experiencing displacement for at least the second time. The rapid escalation left families without vital support as some humanitarian operations have been temporarily suspended. Many families are now seeking shelter in overcrowded camps and centers with limited resources and worsening conditions. In particular limited access to food, clean water, and sanitation are putting the health of children at risk.

Food scarcity is also a growing concern, with bakeries and markets struggling to operate. Public services and critical facilities, including hospitals, power stations, and water supplies, have been disrupted, with some facilities no longer functioning due to a shortage of supplies and staff. Healthcare access has been severely disrupted as health facilities including main hospitals, have been damaged or closed.

As of November 2024, Syria remains one of the largest displacement crises globally, with over 14 million people forcibly displaced since the conflict began in 2011. The children of Syria have endured a series of devastating blows – including ongoing hostilities, widespread displacement, public health emergencies, and the destructive earthquake of 2023. The conflict that escalated in northwest Syria on 26 November 2024, displaced over twenty-four thousand children and put their lives at risk. In 2024, an estimated 16.7 million people in Syria were assessed to need humanitarian aid, making a nine percent increase from the previous year, according to UN agencies. In December 2024, at least 620,000 people were believed to have been killed during the war, and that number is most likely higher. Twelve million Syrians live under conditions of severe food insecurity. More than two-thirds of the displaced are women and children.

Notes

[1] The Mukhabarat is the name of the intelligence services for several countries in the Middle East, including Iraq, Egypt, and Syria. The Iraqi Intelligence Service (IIS) is also known as Mukhabarat. The IIS was responsible for monitoring political parties, opposition groups, and foreign embassies. It also conducted counter-espionage and targeted individuals and groups inside Iraq. Egypt's Military Intelligence (MI) is also known as Mukhabarat Askariya. The MI is a security apparatus believed to control the media. In Syria, the Military Intelligence Directorate (MID) is also known as Mukhabarat. The MID was the military intelligence service of Ba'athist Syria until 2024. It was very influential in Syrian politics. Mukhabarat conducts a variety of activities including surveillance, special operations, monitoring foreign embassies, collecting overseas intelligence, sabotage, subversion, terrorist operations, infiltrating opposition groups abroad, providing disinformation, and maintaining an international network of informants.

[2] The 'cradle of the revolution' refers to a place considered to be the origin or starting points of a revolutionary movement, where the key events and ideas that sparked the revolution first took root and gained momentum: essentially the place where the revolution was born – in Syria that birth was in the city of Daraa.

[3] Executive Order 13338, signed on 5 May 2004, added sanctions and restrictions on Syria in addition to Syria's designation as a State Sponsor of Terrorism in 1979. The Executive Order Implemented the Syria Accountability and Lebanese Sovereignty Restoration Act of 2003 (SAA) and imposed additional measures pursuant to the International Emergency Economic Powers Act (IEEPA) (50 USC 1701 et.seq).

Executive Order 13572, signed on 29 April 2011, blocks the property of Syrian officials and others responsible for the commission of human rights abuses, including those related to repression. Since the uprisings began in March 2011, the US Government has intensely pursued calibrated sanctions to deprive the regime of the resources it needs to continue violence against civilians and to pressure the Syrian regime to end the conflict through a political transition. This Executive Order was the first step taken by the US Government in pursuit of this goal.

Executive Order 13573, signed on 18 May 2011, blocks the property of additional Syrian officials, including President Bashar al-Assad, and of any person determined to be a senior official of the Government of Syria, among other criteria, by the Secretary of the Treasury, in consultation with the Secretary of State.

Executive Order 13582, signed on 18 August 2011, blocks the property of the Government of Syria, provides additional authority for designating individuals and entities, prohibits new investments in Syria by US persons, prohibits the exportation or sale of services to Syria by US persons, prohibits the importation of petroleum or petroleum products of Syrian origin, and prohibits US persons from involvement in transactions involving Syrian petroleum or petroleum products.

Executive Order 13606, signed on 23 April 2012, authorizes sanctions against individuals and entities involved in these activities. This Executive Order was issued in response to the commission of a series of human abuses against the people of Syria and Iran by their governments, facilitated by computer and network disruption, monitoring, and tracking by those governments.

Executive Order 13608, signed on 1 May 2012, authorizes sanctions against such persons. This Executive Order was issued in response to efforts by foreign persons to engage in activities intended to evade US economic and financial sanctions with respect to Syria and Iran.

Chapter Three
Displacement

In 2015, the total number of people displaced around the world was sixty million. A decade later, that number has more than doubled. Some 127 million people are displaced throughout the world… and to put that number in perspective, that is one-third of the population size of the United States of America. Nearly a third of displaced persons are children.

A leading contributor to the unprecedented number of people displaced has been the war in Syria. The pre-war population of Syria was estimated at twenty-two million. Of the pre-war population, some fourteen million have been displaced within the country and another 7.2 million crossed borders into neighboring countries, seeking asylum or placement in refugee camps. Syria is the world's largest displacement crisis.

National databases and media coverage about the Syrian refugee crisis increased markedly bringing considerable attention, to the human costs of the war, the responsibilities of third countries to resettle refugees, pressures forcing refugees to migrate from their host countries, human trafficking, and the exploitation of displaced persons.

The initial understanding of many in the region was that accepting refugees would be a temporary solution to helping those in immediate danger. Türkiye, Jordan, and Lebanon host approximately eighty-four percent of displaced persons from Syria.

The UN High Commissioner for Refugees (UNHCR) curates a database of the estimated number of Syrian refugees and asylum seekers per country. These numbers are gathered from local governments but do not include former refugees who have been resettled. The total number of refugees that a country has received may therefore be higher if a country has accepted or rejected refugees. The data is gathered from the UNHCR Refugees Data Finder, and supplemented with several additional sources.

In 2016, the Regional Refugee and Resilience Plan (3RP) was launched in Türkiye, Lebanon, Jordan, Iraq, and Egypt, to better coordinate humanitarian help between UNHCR, governments, and NGOs. Various nations had made pledges to the UN High Commissioner for Refugees to permanently resettle 170,000 registered refugees.

In the same year, Jordan, Lebanon, and Türkiye negotiated multi-year agreements; namely the Jordan Compact, the Lebanon Compact, and the EU-Türkiye Statement respectively, with international donors that provided material support.

The Jordan Compact is an agreement between Jordan and the international community to help Syrian refugees and Jordan's economy. The compact was announced in 2016 and includes policy changes and investments. Goals improve economic opportunities for refugees, bolster Jordan's economy, provide refugees with settlement and rights, prioritize refugees' safety and well-being, and improve living standards. The Compact intended to allow work permit and business formalization reforms, expand access to the EU market, allow economic activity in refugee camps, and invest in Jordan's special economic zones and other infrastructure projects. For Syrian refugees, there were supposed to be increased employment opportunities, improved access to education, ease the legal barriers and documentation requirements, and empower refugees with more opportunities, mobility, and freedom. However, the implementation faced hurdles.

Negotiated in parallel with the Jordan Compact, the Lebanon Compact was an agreement between the European Union (EU) and Lebanon to improve the lives of Syrian refugees and the communities that host them. The compact was adopted in 2016 and was in effect until 2020. The goals of the Compact were to create a safe and appropriate environment for refugees and displaced people from Syria, to strengthen the economy and infrastructure in Lebanon, to create jobs, to support the stabilization of Lebanon, and to address humanitarian needs in a fair and dignified way. The EU allocated at least US$507 million to Lebanon in 2016 and 2017. Lebanon promised to improve the residency status of

Syrian refugees, and to improve access to education, the labor market, and Lebanese. However, some say the compact was more of a "letter of intent" than an effective policy. They say that the compact's impact faded over time.

The EU-Türkiye Statement, or the EU-Türkiye deal, was a statement of cooperation between the European Union and the Turkish Government signed in March 2016. The statement agreed on three key points: 1)All new irregular migrants crossing from Türkiye to the Greek islands as of 20 March 2016 will be returned to Turkey, 2) For every Syrian returned to Türkiye from the Greek islands, another Syrian will be resettled to the EU, 3) Türkiye will take any means necessary to prevent new sea or land routes for irregular migration opening from Türkiye to the EU. The third point was the most troublesome. Arguments included the fact that Türkiye is not a safe country and those who were returned faced grave human rights violations, as well as the negative impact on human rights in Greece. In return, Türkiye received some US$6.3 billion.

The countries hosting the largest numbers of refugees also introduced several restrictions on new arrivals. Lebanon stopped new registrations and allowed refugees to enter the country only in extreme circumstances Jordan sealed its border with Syria during most of 2016, because of security concerns over ISIS control. NGOs criticized Jordanian authorities for not allowing refugees in and suspended aid to the informal encampments reported on the border.

Reports emerged in 2016 from the Syrian Observatory for Human Rights, the National Coalition of Syrian Revolution and Opposition Forces, Amnesty International, Human Rights Watch, and TGR that Turkish border guards routinely fired at Syrian refugees trying to reach Türkiye. Türkiye has forcibly returned thousands of Syrian refugees to war zones since mid-January 2016. The Turkish Foreign Ministry and President Erdogan have denied it.

For Syrian refugees to have a chance at rebuilding their lives there has to be compassion and mercy. Their plight is through no fault of their own. To make it so difficult for them that they would rather go back to the hellish conditions of war is the polar opposite of compassion and mercy. And it is something that should be outright rejected by humanity.

Approximately 100,000 new third-country resettlement applications were made in 2017. UNHCR received almost one million asylum applications in Europe by August 2017.

In 2018, an estimated 260,000 refugees returned to Syria, and more than 440,000 internally displaced persons returned to their homes to search for family and check on property. However, in the same year, Assad issued the controversial Law No. 10, which enabled the state to confiscate properties from Syrians displaced by the war. Law No. 10 had significant implications for the property rights of Syrians. It was ratified by Bashar al-Assad on 2 April 2018 and amended on 11 November 2018. It is a legal scheme intended to enable the Syrian government to designate land anywhere in the country for redevelopment. Authorities had one week to request a list of property owners from local real estate authorities and land registries. Property owners not on a list from either agency had one year to contest and claim ownership for compensation for the property. Property owners who could not make a claim lost their property.

With more than half the population displaced, and some seven million Syrians outside of the country, it was a legal scheme to further rob Syrians of their possessions – to take their property. And that was assuming that property owners had documents to prove their ownership. However, No. 10 was not the only law that stole from civilians. In 2012, Decree No. 66 allowed Syrian authorities to redevelop areas of unauthorized housing and informal settlements. Decree No 63, authorized the seizure and expropriation of moveable and immovable property belonging to those deemed as terrorists. Decree No. 11 of 2016 halted property registration in areas affected by the "emergency security situation." Law No. 3 of 2018 allowed the removal of "rubble." First, they bombed the country to "rubble", then they deemed everyone who objected as "terrorists" and then they stole all the land.

A few years later, news emerged that the regime was auctioning off lands owned by displaced people to Assad loyalists. The policies were intended to be punishment for citizens not being more loyal to the regime and made it more difficult for refugees to return to Syria.

Refugees do not simply wake up one morning and decide to leave their homes, friends, and family, and choose displacement over peace and stability. The decision to become a refugee is a matter of life and death. These brave people have left everything behind to help their families survive. Many have suffered unimaginable persecution and violence as a result of war, conflict, and discriminative practices led by state terrorism.

Refugee Convention

Refugees are defined by the 1951 UN Convention Relating to the Status of Refugees as "someone who fled his or her home and country owing to a well-founded fear of persecution because of his/her race, religion, nationality, membership in a particular social group, or political opinion". The Refugee Convention, as it is often referred to, describes the international protections afforded to refugees and asylum seekers.

The 1951 Refugee Convention1 is an international agreement that defines the rights of refugees and the obligations of governments to protect them. It was adopted after WW II and is the most comprehensive legal documentation on refugee rights. The convention defines a refugee as someone who has fled their country due to persecution or other threats to their safety. The core principle of the convention is that refugees should not be returned to countries where they face persecution (non-refoulement). The convention outlines the rights of refugees, including access to housing, education, employment, and freedom of movement.

The Geneva Convention on Refugees and its additional Protocol is a multilateral treaty, that sets out the rights of individuals who are granted asylum. The treaty defines the responsibilities of nations that grant asylum; most importantly to the right not to be forcibly returned to their home country, known as non-refoulement.

According to the UN Convention on the Status of Refugees2 Article 33(1): "No Contracting State shall expel or return (refouled) a refugee in any manner whatsoever to the frontiers of territories where his life or freedom would be threatened on account of his race, religion, nationality, membership of a particular social group or political opinion."

The number of migrants requesting international protection has increased exponentially. Every day, men, women, and children flee from persecution, conflict and violence, extreme poverty, hunger, and the consequences of climate crisis and other natural disasters. They risk everything and make one of the most difficult decisions they will ever make – to leave their homes in search of a better life – a safer life.

However, not everyone who is displaced is a refugee. There are several different categories of forcible displacement: Refugees, Asylum Seekers, Internally Displaced Persons, Stateless Persons, and Returnees.

Asylum is an ancient concept. It is the idea that people who are persecuted by their rulers might be protected by another sovereign authority. After the atrocities of WWII, this principle was passed into international law, ensuring that asylum is a fundamental human right and legal status. Asylum status and refugee status are not the same. An asylum seeker is a person who has not yet been legally recognized as a refugee. While anyone can apply for asylum, not everyone who flees to safety will meet the very defined criteria for protection or refugee status. Asylum generally applies to individuals who have a fear of persecution due to their race, religion, nationality, political opinion, or their inclusion in a particular social group. To seek sanctuary, individuals must present themselves at a port of entry (an airport, or an official land crossing), or be in the country in which they are seeking protection. Depending on the path, the length of the asylum process can range from a few months to a few years. Asylum seekers are authorized to remain in the country while their application is pending.

Some displaced persons view the move as an opportunity to start over and to build a new life in a new place to call home – and they look forward to their arrival. Relocation is often a long wait as it comes with a lengthy vetting process, depending on the host country's protocol. But for the committed, the wait is worth the chance to start a new life, free from persecution and violence.

In the US there is this notion among Americans that people in other countries check into a refugee camp, tell the managers that they want to go to America, and voila… they are put on a plane and sent to Ellis Island. Sounds kind of crazy… right? Actually, the US is one of the most difficult countries for a refugee to get to. It is not impossible, but there are a lot of steps in the vetting process3, and it can take several years to get through the process.

Stateless Persons are not recognized by any country and do not have a recognized nationality. This is usually caused by deep discrimination against certain groups. They are prevented from gaining citizenship and excluded from all aspects of services including education, healthcare, or employment.

Returnees are refugees who return to their home country after the exile. Most refugees, about eighty-four percent, stay close to their home country. The main reason for this is that almost everyone dreams of the day when things will change, the conflict and persecution will end, and they can return home. However, this is usually followed by a lengthy stay, in a country where they have no rights and no access to education, healthcare, or permission to work.

Internally Displaced Persons

Internally Displaced Persons (IDPs) are people who have been forced to flee their homes but are still living in their home country; they have not yet crossed borders. Due to more restrictive border management by neighboring countries, many Syrians were unable to leave the country. Displaced persons are the most vulnerable population in conflict.

UN reports indicate that 14.6 million internally displaced people in Syria need some form of humanitarian assistance with as many as five million in critical need. More than twelve million people in Syria cannot find enough to eat daily. At least half a million children are still chronically malnourished.

Millions of people across northern Syria, many of whom are internally displaced, rely on the cross-border flow of food, medicine, and other lifesaving assistance. In 2020, Russia used its veto power to force the UN Security Council to shut down three of the four authorized border crossings into northern Syria, cutting off UN cross-border aid, and making it more difficult to distribute aid. Currently, all of northern Syria relies exclusively on one remaining border crossing.

Northern Syria has been battling a water crisis as a result of several factors including damaged water infrastructure, insufficient rainfall, drought-like conditions, and low levels in the Euphrates River. As a result of water issues, there has been a significant increase in the number of cholera cases. The rapid spread of cholera has also impacted Lebanon. Millions of families live in tents.

There is limited access to healthcare and life-saving services. Destruction of essential infrastructure prohibits safe movement, access to clean water and hygiene, poor sanitation, and limited access to humanitarian resources. There is a risk of further displacement. Food insecurity has reached record-high levels. Food prices continue to rise sharply, basic services remain severely limited. All of this is exacerbated by a desperate economic situation.

An earthquake, measuring 7.8, hit Syria on 6 February 2023. The earthquake and aftershocks in southern Türkiye and northwest Syria deepened the struggles of displaced Syrians. The disaster worsened displacement, elevated hunger levels, malnutrition, and limited access to healthcare and educational support.

Violence Against Displacement Camps

A series of deadly ground attacks and airstrikes were launched against six camps housing internally displaced persons in the Idlib governate in northwest Syria on 6 November 2022. The IDP camp attack in Syria is believed to have been carried out by the Assad regime and Russian forces. The intense shelling included cluster munitions, which are internationally banned and a violation of international humanitarian law.

The Syrian Civil Defense Forces indicated that at least nine people were killed, and some eighty people were injured. Among those killed was Azam Bakir, a four-month-old baby boy. The camps targeted were Maram Camp, Wadi Khaled Camp, Mahtat Mayah Kafr Ruhin Camp, Watan Camp, Murin Village Camp, and B'ieba Camp. Indiscriminate attacks are prohibited by international humanitarian law and may amount to war crimes.

The Maram IDP camp in Kafr Jalis was one of the camps attacked. Yakzan Shishakly, co-founder of the Maram Foundation noted that the camp was established under the supervision of the High Commission for

Refugee Affairs. The camp and its administration are funded by the UN, in collaboration with Maram Foundation.

Maram Foundation has served the displaced population in northwest Syria since 2012. The organization's first camp, the 'Olive Tree Camp' helped more than 28,000 displaced people at the start of the conflict. A decade later, Maram Foundation has assisted more than 1.5 million displaced people throughout northwest Syria.

Crossing Borders

There are 127 million people displaced in the world. The number is overwhelming. There is unprecedented migration around the globe, including record numbers of fatalities of migrants during movement, as attempts to control migration force individuals to take even more dangerous approaches to flee from danger. To resolve the reason why people flee, the global community must address the ways governments and agencies respond to those situations. Governments have a responsibility to protect people and their human rights

The historic number of displaced persons has not only depleted funds allotted for food and basic necessities but has also led to host countries changing their policies to allow refugees to work to support themselves and their families. Since most refugees end up in less developed countries, the increase in population creates an overwhelming burden on the economies and without outside humanitarian support puts countries at risk for economic collapse.

What many hoped would be a situation resolved within a few months has now turned into a very long-term crisis spanning over a decade. And while the Assad regime has fallen, the displacement crisis will not be resolved quickly. The crisis in Syria reaches beyond Syria's borders and impacts the economies, security, education, and health of its neighbors.

In March 2013, some 10,000 people per day were crossing the Syrian border into neighboring countries. Constant aerial bombing by the Syrian military kept approximately 50,000 internally displaced persons from leaving the country. At one point, in 2014, nearly 100,000 people crossed one of Syria's borders every day.

More than a half million Syrians fled to Jordan within the first three years of the war. Just inside the Jordanian border, the Zaatari refugee camp sheltered about 100,000 persons. Nearly twice that amount outside the camp struggled to stay alive.

Millions of refugees who risked their lives in the hope of making a better life in another country have been subjected to accusations of being associated with terrorism, rejected at borders, and held in deplorable conditions, almost as dire as those within the boundaries of their home country.

In the region, refugees predominantly lived in urban, peri-urban, and rural areas, while only about ten percent lived in camps. The majority of refugees live below the poverty line. Hosting countries face overburdened infrastructure in both public and private housing, water, and health, as well as severe disruption of exports through Syria.

Egypt, which does not border Syria, became a major destination for Syrian refugees after 2012, following the election of Mohammed Morsi. During Morsi's presidential term, there were an estimated 70,000 to 100,000 Syrian refugees living in the country. Morsi's government tried to support Syrian refugees by offering residency permits, assistance with finding employment, allowing Syrian children to register in state schools, and access to other public services.

However, following the events relating to the 2013 Egyptian coup, Syrian refugees were met with hostility by Egyptians, who accused them of supporting the Muslim Brotherhood, since the group had close ties with the Syrian opposition and the Free Syrian Army.

The interim government also tightened visa restrictions for Syrian citizens requiring them to obtain a visa and a security clearance before entering Egypt. A study by the Egyptian foreign affairs ministry estimated the country had hosted approximately 500,000 Syrian refugees since the start of the conflict.

Life in Lebanon

Life in Lebanon has not been easy for the refugees displaced by the conflict in Syria. In Lebanon, one in four people is a Syrian refugee. Nearly 74 percent of Syrian refugees in Lebanon are undocumented, which means they are restricted from working, going to school, and receiving access to health care. The situation has resulted in an increasing number of unregistered newborns. Government regulations make it impossible for refugees to obtain or renew residence permits. An increase in security checkpoints prevents men from moving freely, restricting them to their neighborhoods, and without proper documentation, it is nearly impossible to find work to support their families. As a result, many children have been forced to drop out of school to become the primary financial supporters for their families, mostly because children are not as likely to be detained.

Approximately the size of New Jersey, Lebanon has the largest refugee-to-resident ratio in the world. More than a million Syrians and nearly 500,000 Palestinians are registered as refugees in Lebanon. Since Lebanon is not a signatory to the 1951 U.N. Refugee Convention, it does not recognize Syrians as refugees, but rather as foreigners residing in the country.

In 2015 new regulations were implemented in Lebanon that require Syrians to register conditionally through the United Nations for residency. The condition stipulated that they do not work. Alternatively, Syrians could seek Lebanese sponsorship, but that proved very difficult to attain. Once residency is established; the renewal process applies to Syrians over the age of 15 and costs $200 each. Many of the displaced in Lebanon have very few resources and without permission to work, the ability to pay the fee is impossible. As a result, the undocumented population in Lebanon continues to grow.

By the end of 2016, nearly fifty-six percent of Syrians in Lebanon had no valid residency permit. While Lebanon's General Security claims the measures made it easier for Syrians to gain permits, the numbers did not support the claim.

Still, life in Lebanon even for registered Syrians has not been comfortable. Food insecurity is managed with United Nations food rations. Registered male refugees earn an insufficient wage through construction and other eligible work. The cost of health care in Lebanon is unaffordable. Most refugee children are not in school. Those who are in school struggle as many have fallen several grades behind. The trauma of war and conflict has taken a psychological toll on everyone but especially on the children. Without psychological support, the trauma carries over into behavioral issues.

Since many countries, including the United States, have closed their borders to Syrians, Lebanese officials have grown increasingly resentful of the burden placed on their shoulders. Lebanese authorities were against long-term settlement for the Syrian refugees: therefore they have not permitted the establishment of camps. In June 2018, government officials began discussing the return of the displaced back to Syria, although the international community did not completely agree with the idea.

Up to this point, and to its credit, Lebanon has been committed to non-refoulment. As of October 2024, nearly 320,000 Syrian refugees have been repatriated back to Syria. Lebanese officials claim that they are not forcing anyone to return to Syria, but they do not want any outside agencies to discourage any Syrians from returning if they choose to do so.

Children in Conflict

Almost 30 million of the world's refugee population are children. We are talking about an entire generation of stateless children, lost, with insufficient food and shelter, and without access to educational resources. The war has had a devastating impact on the children of Syria. According to UNICEF approximately 7.5 million children in Syria urgently need aid, with millions forced to flee their homes, living in makeshift camps, or overcrowded shelters, on the streets, often without access to basic necessities like food, water, and medical care. Many Syrian children have never known a time without war.

Children are susceptible to ailments brought on by poor sanitation and hygiene, including diarrheal diseases like cholera. They may miss vaccinations and regular health checkups, especially in cutoff areas. In poor housing, cold weather increases the risk of pneumonia and other respiratory infections. Lack of access to healthy foods weakens them further.

The conflict has disrupted the educational system in Syria, with many schools destroyed or closed. As a result, 2.4 million children in Syria have been unable to attend school and many have fallen behind in their education.

The stories of Alan Kurdi and Omran Daqneesh take two different paths. One story is the tragic death of a young toddler and his brother, trying to escape war-torn Syria, and the second is the life of another child; spared from death, but left to endure horrific conditions, trapped in a country of violence and conflict.

In 2015, the lifeless body of two-year-old Alan Kurdi washed ashore on a beach in Türkiye, and the world mourned. The Kurdi family fled Kobani Syria after ISIS seized control of the city. The father arranged passage for him, his wife Rehanna, and their two sons Alan, age two, and Galip, age five. The family boarded a rubber inflatable boat with twelve others. Sixteen people in a rubber dingy made to hold eight. The people were to travel from Bodrum, Turkey to Kos, Greece, a thirty-minute journey across the Mediterranean Sea. A few minutes into the trip, the boat capsized. Rehanna, Galip, and Alan drowned, along with several other people on the raft. The father said that they were wearing life jackets, but they failed to work. Images of Alan being carried away by relief workers continued to flood social media posts for months.

Less than a year after Alan's drowning, another image of a young Syrian boy from the town of Aleppo was shown around the world. Five-year-old Omran Daqneesh was pulled from the rubble after an airstrike hit his family's building in the city of Aleppo. Sitting in the back of an ambulance, covered in dust debris, and blood, his face, as did Alan's body on the shoreline, became the plight of children in the war in Syria.

With their families struggling to make ends meet, many children have been forced to work in dangerous and exploitative conditions to help support their families. Both government forces and armed groups have been known to recruit children to fight in the conflict putting them in harm's way and robbing them of their childhood.

Children are more vulnerable to sexual abuse and exploitation in the unfamiliar and overcrowded conditions in refugee camps and informal tent settlements. There is an increasing concern about the exploitation of female refugees. Families desperate for income may be more prone to arrange marriages for their young daughters in exchange for dowries.

Life for young Syrian girls has been very difficult. Many are at risk for sexual abuse and being married off to older men. Multiple reports claim that young girls are being "purchased" by older (sixty years old and older) Qatari and Saudi men. The exploitation of Syrian women and girls is deplorable and unacceptable. International law demands the protection of all refugees.

Refoulment in Jordan

There is evidence to support that the number of refugees entering Jordan may be decreasing as the country has been accused of forcibly sending refugees back to Syria. According to a report issued by Amnesty International, in 2012 hundreds of refugees were deported by Jordan back to Syria. Jordan has made no distinction between national origins and sending back undocumented workers.

Part of the problem lies in the fact that the impoverished conditions inside, as well as outside the refugee camps have forced many to seek employment, which has created feelings of open hostility toward the refugees. Syrian refugees are blamed for the lack of jobs as well as the increase in the Kingdom's unemployment rate which is fourteen percent. Jordan's Ministry of Labor said that for refugees to work they must have the appropriate documentation and if they do not, they are breaking the law and are, therefore, deportable.

Officially, Jordan claims that anyone who has returned to Syria has done so voluntarily, although interviews conducted with returned refugees do not support that. In a country ripped apart by civil war, it is inconceivable that Jordan, or any other country for that matter would send refugees that have successfully made the safe passage, back into a war zone. There have been multiple reports of late-night raids by police, the threat of beatings, and Syrian refugees held in clandestine centers and being dumped at the border; events that violate international law.

More than US$750 million - has been awarded to Jordan to help with the costs incurred in refugee housing and basic necessities. While international charity organizations wait to bring in additional aid that would help the refugees, the Jordanian government will not allow the aid to pass which in turn puts the people most in need at an even higher risk for exploitation.

Living in Poverty

The vast majority of refugees live below the poverty line. In Lebanon, most households were below $85 monthly per capita. In Türkiye, ninety percent were below $100 and seventy percent below $50 monthly. Average monthly expenditures were estimated in 2020 at $104 in Lebanon and $55 in Southeast Türkiye.

Underemployment and low wages are widespread. Many rely on less sustainable sources, food vouchers, taking credits, or borrowing money mostly from friends and relatives, less frequently from shops, and rarely from landlords. In Lebanon, ninety percent of households were in debt $850 on average. Because of this, refugees face difficulties accessing services and providing food, housing, healthcare, and other basic needs for their families.

In January 2019, the UN said that fifteen displaced Syrian children, thirteen of them under one year old, had died due to cold weather and inadequate medical care. In addition, several days of strong winds, heavy rains, snow, and subsequent flooding caused the death of one child and led to the destruction of more than three hundred sixty sites housing 11,300 refugees in Lebanon. In Syria, families fleeing the conflict in Hajin were left in the cold for days, without shelter or basic supplies.

In January 2021, at least 22,000 civilians lost their temporary homes as heavy rains flooded, and snow destroyed over four-thousand tents at displacement camps in northern Idlib and western Aleppo.

Refugees live primarily within hosting communities in rented houses or informal tent settlements and sub-standard dwellings. Only about ten percent live in formal camps. In Lebanon eighty-five percent pay rent, seventy-one percent live in residential buildings, twelve percent in non-residential structures, and seventeen percent in informal tent settlements. A quarter of homes are overcrowded. In southern Türkiye, ninety-six percent of the refugees living outside of camps pay rent, sixty-two percent live in rented apartments, twenty-eight percent live in unfinished buildings, and one percent live in tents.

Refugees are commonly charged a higher rate compared to local people, especially for sub-standard conditions. In Lebanon, a monthly average of $53 for keeping tents on land, to $250 for a non-shared apartment or house, often excluding water and electricity. Few refugees have residency permits in Lebanon, mainly due to their cost, creating difficulties at checkpoints when moving in search of jobs.

Earning opportunities for refugees are predominately informal, principally due to governments issuing few work permits. Barriers include quotas, fees, long and cumbersome paperwork, and discrimination by employers. In Türkiye, even after reforms opened the labor market the number of refugees in a single workplace could not exceed ten percent. Employers pay work permit fees of $180 per year. While there is an exception for seasonal work, it requires a separate application and still requires being registered for at least six months. At most several thousand permits had been issued. Refugees are thus overwhelmingly employed informally. Jobs are often seasonal, and employment rates differ widely between winter and summer.

Notes

[1]For read the Convention in its entirety and to learn more about refugees visit:https://www.thegenocidereport.org/1951-refugee-convention/

[2]For more information on the UN Protocol on the Status of Refugees please visit: https://www.thegenocidereport.org/protocol-relating-status-refugees/

[3]The vetting process for refugees is a lengthy procedure. The US has one of the most intense and stringent vetting processes, more so than many other countries, taking between two to five years for approval and resettlement. Refugees are subjected to severe scrutiny which includes multiple interviews, fingerprint screening, iris scans, and background checks across multiple agencies including the State Department, the FBI, Homeland Security, and US Immigration, all in addition to the initial interview and registration with the United Nations.

Chapter Four
Sednaya

Nineteen miles north of Damascus, in Rif Dimashq, near the ancient monastery where Christians and Muslims prayed for centuries, is one of the worst places in Syria. Sednaya Military Prison was a death camp, operated by the Assad regime. The prison was under the jurisdiction of the Minister of Defense and operated by the Syrian Military Police. A former guard at Sednaya said, "Sednaya is the end of life; it is the end of humanity."

Sednaya was used to hold thousands of prisoners of both genders, including civilian detainees, anti-government protesters, and international prisoners held by other government agencies for extraordinary rendition. Most of the prisoners were civilians suspected of opposing the government. It is where the state quietly and methodically tortured and executed detainees. However, over the years, violations against detainees increased dramatically in magnitude and severity.

Before being transferred to Sednaya, detainees typically spent months or years in other detention facilities. The prison often served as the final destination for prisoners after extended stays in facilities. In some cases, protesters were taken directly to Sednaya. A wide variety of brutal practices were carried out in the prison ranging from perpetual beatings, sexual assaults, rapes, burnings, decapitations, and the use of tools such as the hinged boards known as "flying carpets". There are well-documented cases of detainees being killed after being repeatedly tortured and systematically deprived of food, water, medicine, and medical care, as well as the government's use of more than forty torture techniques in its prisons.

Since 2011, thousands of people have been extrajudicially executed in mass hangings, conducted in the dark of night, in the utmost secrecy. In January 2023, the Syrian Observatory for Human Rights estimated that since 2011, at least 30,000 detainees were killed by the Assad regime in Sednaya. It is unfathomable that these large-scale and systematic practices were not authorized at the highest levels of the Syrian government. The violations at the prison amount to crimes against humanity and war crimes.

The prison consisted of two buildings: the red building and the white building, and included a less accessible, underground system that extended three levels below. Many of the severely abused prisoners were kept in the lower levels. The larger, red-radial-shaped building was used to hold civilians and political prisoners, many of whom were arrested since the beginning of the uprisings in 2011. The white L-shaped building held officers and soldiers in the Syrian military who were considered disloyal to Assad.

There were at least two salt rooms in the prison. Located on the first floor of the red building, the rooms were used to store salt for de-icing the roads. However, they also served as mortuaries to preserve dead bodies in the absence of refrigerated morgues. Interviews with previous detainees indicated that the deceased body was left inside a cell with other prisoners for two to five days, and then taken to the salt room.

Until the prison was photographed by one of its liberators on 8 December 2024, no images of Sednaya prison aside from satellite photos existed. In May 2017, the US State Department accused the Syrian government of operating a crematorium at Sednaya. Based on satellite photographs taken over several years beginning in 2013, the pictures indicated building modifications that were interpreted as consistent with a crematorium. The US determined that the prison was using the ovens to dispose of bodies and destroy evidence of war crimes, although they could not prove its existence. However, witnesses claimed they knew of bodies being burned, and had detected suspicious odors.

Rebels also discovered an iron press used to compress the remains of executed prisoners. The torture, forced disappearance, and extermination carried out at Sednaya were perpetrated as part of an attack against the civilian population that was widespread, systematic, and carried out in furtherance of state policy.

Testimonies of former prisoners indicated that detainees rarely saw daylight and were forced to cover their eyes with their hands whenever a guard entered the cell. Consequently, they developed an acute association with sound, becoming familiar with the smallest sounds, especially footsteps, doors opening and locking, and water dripping in the pipes. Sound became the instrument by which detainees navigated and assessed their environment.

Former detainees recollected, that a person can build an image based on the sounds they hear. For example, you can tell the person by the sound of their footsteps. You know the food times by the sound of the bowl. If you hear screaming, you know new prisoners have arrived. When there is no screaming you know they are adapted to Sednaya. The acoustics in the prison were such that when one person was being tortured, it was like everyone was being tortured. There was no way to escape it.

Prisoners came from all sectors of Syrian society. Many had demonstrated longtime political dissension, including human rights advocates and activists, journalists, doctors, educators, lawyers, humanitarian aid workers, and students. The people at greatest risk of torture, and death were those perceived to oppose the regime in some way.

Murder, torture, enforced disappearances, and extermination have been carried out at Sednaya. The prison regularly carried out mass hangings several times a week, killing as many as fifty people in each event. Before the executions, the victims were condemned to death in sham trials that lasted between one to three minutes. Prison authorities referred to the mass executions as the "party". They collected the victims from their cells in the afternoon. The detainees were told they were being transferred to a civilian prison. Instead, they were taken to a cell in the basement of the red building where they were severely beaten for several hours. Then, in the middle of the night, they were blindfolded and transferred in delivery trucks to the white building. The victims were taken to the basement and hanged to death.

Since its inception, the prison has been a black mark on the human rights map. The inhuman treatment of detainees held at Sednaya, and other government-run detention centers, has included extermination. Extermination, as defined by the Rome Statute of the International Criminal Court is the intentional and systematic killing of a civilian population, with the intent to destroy part of that group. The Court lists the deprivation of access to food and medicine, and using torture or other severe physical violence as methods of mass killing. Extermination is an atrocity crime – a crime against humanity.

Project: Ceasar

In 2014, Sednaya became part of the international discourse on human rights abuses in Syria when a photographer with the Syrian Military Police, known by the pseudonym Caesar, defected and fled the country with the help of the NGO, the Coalition for a Democratic Syria. The Ceasar Report, as it became known, was a cache of more than 55,000 photographs of the torture and death of at least 11,000 victims. The victims were detainees in Assad's prisons and detention centers, including Tishreen, Mezza Air Force Branch, and Sednaya. While he did not claim to have witnessed any torture or executions, he confessed to having taken the photographs of killed detainees and smuggled them out of the country on flash drives.

The process was that when detainees were killed, the body was given a reference number that corresponded to the branch of the security service responsible for the detention and death. The bodies were taken to a military hospital. Once there, a doctor made the official pronouncement of death. The authorities took the victims to the hospital to avoid raising concerns that the prison was torturing detainees to death, extrajudicially killing them, or carrying out extermination. Especially since all of that and more, are a violation of international law – the fewer questions the better. Families were told that the cause of death was a heart attack or breathing problems.

At this point, Ceasar would photograph the corpse, including the reference number. He noted that there could be as many as fifty bodies a day to photograph. Ceasar observed the reason he photographed the executed detainees was to produce a death certificate without the families being required to see the body, thereby avoiding having to give a truthful account of their deaths. But also to confirm to the Assad regime that the individuals had been executed. After the bodies were photographed, they were buried in mass graves in rural areas.

The photographs revealed images of tortured, bloodied, and bruised persons. Most of the victims were young men and many corpses were emaciated from being starved. Some had their eyes gouged out – they had no eyes. Some bodies were charred. The skin of others had been flayed. And still others showed signs of strangulation or electrocution. Very few images did not show signs of an injury that accounted for death. A fatal injury to the back of the body would not be represented in the photographs because only the front of the bodies and faces were photographed. And there are many ways in which an individual may be killed with minimal effort, and not present external evidence of the manner of death.

In July 2014, Caesar testified before the US Congress. The photographs were given to the FBI and the office of the American ambassador at large for war crimes issues, Stephen J Rapp. There is no doubt about the authenticity of these photographs. The FBI found no trace of forgery.

A sample of the photos was submitted to an inquiry team for examination. The inquiry team consisted of three former prosecutors at the criminal tribunals for the former Yugoslavia and Sierra Leone. Sir Desmond de Silva QC, former chief prosecutor of the Special Court for Sierra Leone, Sir Geoffery Nice QC, the former lead prosecutor of former Yugoslavia president Slobodan Milosevic, and Professor David Crane, who indicted President Charles Taylor of Liberia at the Sierra Leone court, carefully and rigorously examined the photographs, and determined that they were most compelling. It was determined that the evidence presented in the cache of photos was incontrovertible proof, the type of evidence that did not exist before, of the crimes of the Assad regime.

A thirty-one-page report, commissioned by a firm of London solicitors on behalf of Qatar, and authored by the inquiry team was made available to the United Nations, governments, and human rights groups. The UN and independent human rights groups have documented abuses by both Bashar al-Assad's government and rebels, but experts say this evidence is more detailed and on a far larger scale than anything else that has yet emerged from the crisis.

In any war crime trial, the prosecutor argues that the evidence overall indicates that the pattern of behavior would likely have to be approved at the highest level of government – ultimately the head of state. However, whether you can go beyond that and say it must be approved by the head of state is a bit more difficult. But the widespread and systematic torture and violence in this situation do portend government control. The fact that the Syrian authorities ordered the pictures to be taken to verify that the prison military had killed the person they reported as dead is an indication of the regime's intentional, systematic, and repeated crimes against its population. The photos are direct evidence of what happened to 11,000 people who had disappeared. These were human beings who had been tortured, executed, and disposed of.

In 2015, Ceasar presented his images to the National Holocaust Museum in Washington, DC. Ten images were exhibited in the Museum's Genocide Prevention Center, seeking to learn how best to preserve and archive the images and preserve them for future prosecution. The images were also on display at the United Nations Headquarters in New York. And while the photos were difficult to look at, they left no question that the Assad regime was complicit. Killing of this magnitude could not be carried out without the top echelon of government not knowing it was happening.

The displaying of Ceasar's photos came as the world's attention had shifted from Assad's brutalities to the threat of extremist groups such as the Islamic State (ISIS). However, in 2014, the Assad regime killed 32,500 people, seventy-five percent of whom were civilians. In contrast, ISIS killed 3,657, eighty-five percent of whom were military targets. It is impossible to get away from the fact that the Assad regime deliberately used horrific force and treatment against its people. And it is not a difficult reach, to assume that the reason was that Assad had watched the fall of dictators in Tunisia, Libya, and Egypt – and he was determined that none of that was going to happen in Syria. Assad instilled fear in the people to keep them too afraid to react.

A proposed Security Council resolution1 to refer Syria to the International Criminal Court was struck down by two vetoes in May 2014. Then US Ambassador to the UN, Samantha Power said, "Today was about accountability for crimes so extensive and deadly that they had few equals in modern history." But the vote was also about accountability of the Security Council. It was then and still is, the Council's responsibility to stop atrocities when it can, and to ensure that the perpetrators are held accountable. The judicial process gives the victims of atrocities a voice.

However, in a radical change in strategy, UN war crimes investigations published the names of suspects involved in perpetuating the atrocities committed throughout the Syrian war. In the case of Assad, he's responsible for the kind of things that have led to the rise of the extremists. We cannot forget that, even if getting to accountability is not easy.

Calls for Assad and others to face justice at the international criminal court in The Hague floundered on the problems that Syria is not a member of the court, and that the required referral by the UN Security Council might not be supported by the US and UK or would be blocked by Russia, Syria's close ally.

Former UK Foreign Secretary William Hague said the report offered further evidence of the systematic violence and brutality visited upon the people of Syria by the Assad regime. Hague said we must continue to press for action on all human rights violations in Syria and for accountability for those who perpetrate them.

The cache of photos lends to the sadistic nature of the Assad regime. In Pinochet's Chile, the bodies of the victims of the regime floated down the river in a public display. In Argentina during the Dirty War, the regime used death flights to drop bodies out over the ocean to conceal the evidence of its crimes. But in Syria, Assad tortured his victims to death, then numbered and photographed them to preserve the evidence of his crime. The psychological nature of this is not unlike a serial killer returning to the scene of the crime to recall the victim's suffering. It really is an incredible amount of evidence that we hope to see used against Bashar al-Assad one day in The Hague.

The Stories

In Sednaya, torture was not used to force a detainee to confess, as it is used in branches of the security forces, but rather as a method of punishment and degradation. The most common form of torture used at Sednaya was serial and brutal beatings. Former detainees said the beatings they received were sometimes, so severe that they caused life-long damage and disability, or death.

Torture methods in Sednaya varied. Rami, a former detainee described an interrogation technique frequently used by the guards. He said the guards had him stand on a barrel with his wrists bound. The rope was pulled up and over a support so that his arms were pulled up over his head. Then they removed the barrel so that his weight was no longer supported. He said his feet were dangling in the air. With his arms in a stressed position, the guards began beating him with sticks, hitting him everywhere. One of his shoulders was dislocated during the beating. Then they burned him all over his body with cigarettes. He said it felt like they were cutting him with a knife. He said the guards used other methods of torture including leaving people in stress positions while beating them or torturing them with electricity.

Mazen was first arrested in 2011 for organizing a pro-democracy protest. He was arrested again in 2012 and in 2013. He was detained for more than a year and a half and at one point was forced into a small space with 170 others. Mazen was beaten, sexually assaulted, and tortured by regime henchmen, trying to force a confession. Mazen carried permanent physical and psychological scars of the regime's abuse. He was eventually released and exiled to the Netherlands where he became an internationally known speaker of the atrocities committed by Bashar al-Assad's forces and became an advocate for accountability and justice. In February 2020, Mazen was tricked into returning to Syria. He was arrested in Damascus by security services. On 9 December 2024, Mazen's body was discovered during the liberation of Sednaya. He was severely disfigured, wrapped in a bloody cloth. He had been dead only a few days.

Former detainees described specific memories and events from their time in Sednaya. Some flashes of recollections had been obscured by violence and trauma. Due to severe trauma, many released detainees had forgotten their names, and some could not speak. They were taken to a local mosque for identification, and photos were placed on social media, and also with the Association of Detainees and the Missing in Sednaya Prison2.

New detainees were subjected to what was known as the "welcome party", during which they were systematically beaten. One former detainee, a lawyer from Homs named Samir, described the process… "The soldiers practiced their hospitality with each new group of detainees during the welcome party. The men were stripped and beaten. A few of the younger boys were taken to solitary cells and beaten further. You could tell the beatings stopped when the screaming stopped."

Omar was a professor at Damascus University who was arrested in 2014 and sent to Sednaya. In an interview, he recalled his entrance to the prison: "I was blindfolded the whole time, but I tried to see through the fold. I could see the image of the person hitting and kicking me. He hit me repeatedly with a metal object. When I fell to the floor, all I could see was blood. After one hit, I lost sense of what was happening. And then there was pain."

During the entrance to the prison, detainees were shoved to the ground. The guards used different instruments for the beatings including regular electric cables, various plastic water pipes, and metal bars. One such weapon used was electric cables with exposed copper wire ends that had little hooks that tore the skin. Another torture instrument used was called the "tank belt", made out of a tire that was cut into strips. The device made a very specific sound, like a small explosion.

Aziz, a former guard who worked at Sednaya for a few months in 2016, said when new prisoners arrived, they were subjected to an initiation. He said that the guards often looked for the weaker of the arrivals and targeted them. Aziz said that some of the guards were especially brutal. He said on more than one occasion he had to intervene to prevent the guards from killing prisoners before they were even admitted to the prison.

Former detainee, Samer recalled the small opening near the bottom of his cell door, just large enough for him to squeeze his head through. The guards pulled it through so that his throat was pressed against the edge. Then, the guards stood on his head with their weight so that the edge of the metal cut his throat until blood flowed.

Omar al-Shogre is the director for detainee affairs at the Syrian Emergency Task Force, a US-based nonprofit established in March 2011 to support the opposition. Omar was arrested multiple times between 2011 and 2013. He was held at Branch 215 where he was subjected to daily physical and psychological torture including the pulling of his fingernails, electric shock, and beatings with metal objects and cables. Omar was eventually released to his mother after she paid a $15,000 bribe. On the day of his release, he weighed eighty-two pounds. He had contracted tuberculosis and was starved. He credits his survival to older prisoners.

Abdul, a former detainee, revealed that detainees were raped and forced to rape each other. He said: "They beat me until I collapsed on the ground. Then they kicked me with their boots on my hip, at the place where I had hip surgery. They kicked me until I passed out. When I woke up I was in the cell. My trousers had been pulled down and my abaya was open and pulled up. My body was sore, and my back was bleeding. The men had raped me. There was overwhelming pain everywhere."

Another former detainee Hassan said "The guards made the prisoners take off their clothes and touch each other in sensitive places and rape each other too. I went through this only one time, but I heard about it happening frequently to others."

A lawyer who worked with prisoners in Hama said: "Seventy-five percent of people who go into Sednaya do not come out alive. It is a field court, where most 'judges' are from the secret police. If a prisoner was sent to Sednaya, they most likely died there."

Mus'ab is a Syrian teenager and member of the banned organization the Muslim Brotherhood. Mus'ab lived in exile with his mother in Saudi Arabia until 2002, when they returned to Syria. His mother was concerned that their return would create problems for Mus'ab because of his political opinions. However, the Syrian embassy in Saudi Arabia had assured her that it would not be a problem.

But shortly after they returned to Syria, Mus'ab was arrested and sentenced by the Syrian security forces on 24 July 2002. At the time of his arrest, he was only fourteen years old. Based on the assessment that Mus'ab did not receive a fair trial, his age at the time of arrest, the fact he was tortured, and sentenced by the Supreme State Security Court to six years in prison, despite no substantial evidence of a crime, the UN Working Group on Arbitrary Detention deemed his arrest as arbitrary and demanded his release. Still, the authorities would not release Mus'ab from custody.

In 2004, the Syrian Human Rights Committee reported that people were being arrested for political reasons. The report indicated that suspected individuals were not offered human rights defenders or lawyers – as was the case with Mus'ab. Hundreds of prisoners remained in long detention, without due process, without trial, or subjected to enforced sentences after unfair trials. The Syrian Human Rights Committee also determined that no respect was given to the poor health condition of prisoners and that conditions were quite severe.

Tareq is a Syrian teenager from Idlib. He was detained during protests in 2013. During several years of imprisonment, he stated that he had gone through eleven Syrian prisons. Sednaya was the last prison. He described the events in Sednaya, beginning with the "welcome party" in which new detainees were beaten with metal parts from a tank. Tareq said that one officer beat ten new detainees. He stated that for fifteen days he couldn't open his eyes or get up. After a month in Sednaya, he was charged with terrorism and taken to trial. He said the trial lasted five seconds. He contracted a bacterial infection which led to breathing problems in Sednaya.

Mohammad was arrested for participating in a peaceful non-violent protest. The former prisoner said that at the first prison he was sent to, Branch 215, the guards interrogated prisoners through torture. Then he was sent to Sednaya. He said detainees at Sednaya were forced to choose which family member was to be killed or they would be killed themselves. Mohammad said people were moved to Sednaya to die.

Diab, a former detainee had been accused of forming a youth opposition group. He was arrested in 2006 and released in 2011 after a general amnesty. "We had the feeling that the prison would rebel at any moment because the conditions were unbearable." He was right. Prisoners reached a point where it was better to die than to exist in Sednaya. The violently controlling policies of the corrupt prison director led prisoners to revolt.

At least two rebellions within Sednaya were issued in response to the policies of the prison director, Ali Kher Bek. Bek was very strict and harsh with detainees. He exploited the prison conditions for inmates by terminating visits and cutting electricity for long periods. When the inmates raised their concerns, Bek hit them with more restrictions. In March 2008, a fight broke out between a prisoner and a guard. Bek took his rage out on the prisoners. The next morning, he and the security forces walked through the prison. The security forces dragged prisoners out of their cells and tortured them. Detainees shouted "Allahu Akbar" (God is Great) and banged on the doors. The altercation turned into a rebellion and spun out of control. Security forces used tear gas and fired into the air to intimidate the prisoners. Prisoners ran to the roof and burned whatever they could find to signal for help.

After one day of the rebellion, the security forces regained control of Sednaya. The government negotiated an agreement with the prisoners to provide fair trials, permit family visitations, increase daily break times, enhance the living conditions, and increase medical care. The government kept its agreement for a time, but less than four months later, in July 2008, once again, the prison director Bek launched a new offensive to discipline the prisoners.

Fights broke out between the prisoners and military police until the prisoners overpowered them. The prisoners took 1,500 military police hostage. Outside security forces opened fire and killed everyone in a group trying to escape. Some prisoners and hostages made it to the roof, but military forces opened fire on them and killed thirty military police hostages and the prisoners. Ten of the military police hostages were killed by prisoners. Six military police committed suicide for fear of being killed by the prisoners. Military reinforcements from Damascus arrived in Sednaya and laid siege. The siege lasted ten days. The Assad government agreed to evacuate the injured to Tishreen Hospital, where they were tortured to death.

Osman, a liberated prisoner, recounted the details of a "welcome party" that included men and women detainees. New arrivals were delivered in a truck used to transport frozen meats – it was called the "meat fridge." The prisoners had no idea where they were until the doors opened. Immediately the beatings began with metal bars and cables. That was followed by "security checks" during which everyone was subjected to rape and sexual assault by the guards. The women in that group were passed from guard to guard and then the male prisoners were told to rape the women or be beaten. Several of the men took the beatings. Osman recollected that as they waited for their turn, they heard the sounds of the beatings and the people falling out of the truck. "Everyone was screaming."

Karim and Yusuf spent the first seven months of their imprisonment at Sednaya underground in a freezing cold solitary confinement cell, designed to hold one person, but was used to hold fifteen men. The men were forced to take turns sitting down in the cramped room. They recounted that for weeks at a time, the water was cut off. They were forced to drink from the toilet gutter. The sound of water dripping caused hallucinations and bouts of panic and hysteria.

For Ibrahim, who lost five years of his life in Sednaya, and was liberated by rebels in December 2024, he wants the prison to stand as a lasting reminder to the generations to come of the horrors inflicted on the people. He said "The world should know it is the worst place on earth.

Liberation of Sednaya

On 8 December 2024, Sednaya Military Prison was taken over by opposition forces as they advanced into Damascus. The prison administration agreed to surrender the prison to the rebel forces, in exchange for their safe withdrawal. Following the takeover, the remaining inmates in the white building of the prison were released from the facility. It took the liberating forces several more days to break into and free inmates from the larger red building in the prison.

The rebel forces also discovered underground cells beneath the main prison building where dozens of men were confined in darkness. Prisoners trapped in tunnels under the buildings called for help, prompting the rebels to break through concrete barriers to free them. The cells contained water-soaked blankets and plastic bottles used for urine storage. Search efforts by the Syrian Emergency Task Force determined that no additional sealed areas or victims were left. For the first time since 1987, Sednaya had no prisoners.

Sednaya represented the repressiveness of the Assad regime – both father and son – but it lends to the exceptional cruelty of Bashar al-Assad. His regime used torture, sexual assault, and mass execution to control his people. The fact he did these things, and he was a medical doctor places him on the same stage as Mengele3.

Many detainees were overwhelmed to be released. The initial reaction was disbelief and confusion. Still, others did not want to leave their cells, afraid it was a trick to be beaten and tortured. Videos and images appeared on social media showing the imprisoned people, including families and children.

In the women's section of the prison, many women had been imprisoned along with their children. The women were afraid. The rebels identified themselves and told them Bashar al-Assad had fallen, and urged the prisoners to come out of their cells. They told them they were free to leave.

Some prisoners had been detained for decades in Sednaya and did not know that Bashar al-Assad's father, Hafez, had died twenty-four years earlier – they did not know how long they had been in Sednaya or what year it was. Some did not know who Bashar al-Assad war. They believed that Hafez was still in power, and mistook rebel troops for invading Ba'athist Iraqi forces under Saddam Hussein coming to liberate them.

Witnesses reported helicopters landing at Sednaya Military Prison on 7 December 2024, a day before rebel forces arrived. The helicopters were used to evacuate guards and high-valued prisoners. After the fall of the prison, Hayat Taher al-Sham, leader of the Syrian opposition (HTS), published a list of names of escaped prison staff. Their names are now among the most wanted fugitives in Syria, second only to the members of the Assad family.

According to Fadel Abdul Ghany, director of the Syrian Network for Human Rights, approximately 2,000 prisoners emerged from Sednaya when it was liberated, though questions remain about the fate of thousands more who were believed to have been held there. Video from the liberation of Sednaya showed numbered cells that had dozens of prisoners each, littered with debris, clothing, and belongings.

The Association of Detainees and the Missing in Sednaya Prison stated it had documentation showing about 4,300 detainees as of 28 October 2024. Only half of that number was liberated.

Notes

[1] Referral of Syria to International Criminal Court Fails as Negative Votes SC 11407 https://press.un.org/en/2014/sc11407.doc.htm

[2] The Association of Detainees and the Missing in Sednaya Prison (ADMSP) is an organization that seeks justice for victims of the Syria prison. The ADMSP was formed in 2017 by survivors, victims, and families of those detained at Sednaya Prison. The ADMSP has partnered with Amnesty International, Impunity Watch, and the Geneva Academy. The ADMSP advocates for uncovering the truth and achieving justice for those detained in Sednaya Prison. The group has called for the transitional Syrian authorities to preserve evidence of atrocities committed by the former government. https://www.admsp.org/en/

[3] Josef Mengele was a German Schutzstaffel (SS) physician. Known as the "angel of death" by his victims, Mengele conducted inhumane medical experiments on prisoners in the Auschwitz death camp. He supervised the arrival of incoming prisoners and determined whether they were sent to forced labor or immediate extermination. He experimented on live Jewish prisoners, Romani, persons with disabilities, and twins. Mengele absconded from justice after the war and moved to South America, first to Paraguay, and then to Brazil, where he reconnected with a former member of the Nazi party, Wolfgang Gerhard in 1985. When Gerhard died, dental records revealed it was Josef Mengele. He had assumed Gerhard's identity.

Chapter Five
Missing and
Disappeared

Fifty-four years of Assad family rule in Syria is over. As Syrians grasp the full meaning of that, the interim government shifts toward geopolitics and what is next for the country. However, there is a grim reality that lingers… what happened to the hundreds of thousands of people still missing? For the families of the missing and disappeared, finding their loved ones is the priority.

The death toll in Syria is believed to be 600,000 or more. Estimates by the Syrian Civil Defense (the White Helmets), place the number of people missing from 100,000 to 200,000, but the number is likely much higher. In Syria, persons are missing as a consequence of summary executions, arbitrary detention, and abductions, as well as persons kidnapped for other nefarious reasons, as a result of thirteen years of war. Tens of thousands were arrested by Syrian security services and imprisoned without cause. Tens of thousands died while in government

95

custody. Since 2011, the Assad regime "disappeared" hundreds of thousands of people as a means of intimidating anyone who opposed it.

When questioned in 2019 regarding the number of unexplained missing persons, former Syrian Ambassador Bassam Sabbagh said that Syria had addressed the issue of missing persons. According to Sabbagh, "All claims of disappearance submitted to law enforcement authorities had been independently investigated under Syrian law and based on information and resources." According to Sabbagh, less than 10,000 people were missing… but we know that is not the truth.

Syrians and non-Syrians are missing inside Syria. There are missing journalists, humanitarian workers, and medical personnel. There are fighters from more than sixty countries who are missing in Syria. Iraqis are missing inside Syria. There are also Yazidi populations that are both missing inside and outside of Syria. Some children have been orphaned and can no longer find their parents. Children need to have their familial links restored, to find their family again. People are missing as a result of sarin gas attacks and chlorine barrel bomb attacks. Some people went missing as a result of the fighting, as a result of the destruction, as a result of human rights abuses, including enforced disappearance.

People who fled the conflict have gone missing along the migrant route. Each person has a very painful story. A lot of families lost not only one person but many family members. Refugees oftentimes go missing in groups. The dangerous crossings of the Mediterranean Sea have claimed many unidentified persons. Criminal enterprises prey upon displaced populations, refugees, and migrants particularly human trafficking rings. We need to find the answers to these questions so that families can be reunited, and have closure. There must be protocols put in place to prevent further disappearance; and any further instances of people going missing with full respect to international humanitarian law1 (IHL) and human rights law obligations.

It is critical that any process to locate the missing and investigate the disappeared is led by Syria and that the authorities place the interests and rights of the families of the missing at the center. It needs to be a united effort, especially between the new government and families of the missing, but also include the resources of humanitarian organizations to assist where it can. An effective process will establish the fate of missing persons, secure the human rights of survivors and victims, and lay the groundwork for holding the perpetrators accountable.

There is a window of opportunity to achieve an objective that was unimaginable three months ago… to locate and identify the hundreds of thousands of Syrians who are still missing. Understanding that the majority of missing persons are men, Syrian women must play a leading role in driving the missing persons process. Women must be central to the strategy that is formed.

Preserving the evidence is crucial. The war in Syria and the atrocities committed by Bashar al-Assad is one of the most widely documented in history, largely due to the many brave persons on the ground in Syria, who have collected data and recorded the atrocities committed over the last decade. In many cases risking their lives to do so. This documentation will be essential now to hold Assad and all those who committed crimes, in future prosecutions. But it will also be invaluable in finding the missing.

Evidence

The search for missing persons is a complex multilayered long-term process. It will require the support and participation of and coordination with families and authorities. Families of those who are missing or disappeared have gone years, even decades of living with uncertainty of what happened to their loved ones. The families have worked tirelessly to advocate on their behalf.

Appropriate measures must be taken to preserve the evidence that will shed light on the circumstances regarding the missing status of persons. In cases where they are deceased, the circumstances of their deaths need to be known. We need this to bring those responsible to justice.

Authorities need to take measures to protect and preserve vital records and primary source data, remove them from public circulation, and protect them from loss, damage, or compromise. It is imperative to take measures to protect mass graves and sites of vital importance.

As detention centers and prisons are opened and detainees released, authorities must secure and preserve archives, all records including arrest, detention lists, detainee transfers, court, hospital, executions, death records, burial records, information about potential or known burial sites, and any other official documentation that can help clarify the fate and whereabouts of missing persons.

All stakeholders must cooperate. Any process to locate these people and investigate their disappearance must be transparent. Connecting people and data is mandatory if we are to close the overwhelming number of missing person cases. Collecting documentation of violations from all available sources, storing documentation and findings in a secure database, cataloging data according to human rights standards, and analyzing findings using legal expertise and big data methodologies are essential to reaching objectives. Identifying patterns helps in building hypotheses about the possible fates and whereabouts of individual victims for identification.

Data processes include collecting documentation on missing persons through interviews with witnesses, family members, and former affiliates, adding to other evidence, satellite imagery, records from security services, judicial apparatus, open-source documentation, and documentation from exhumations. Using forensic methods to investigate missing persons and mass graves, including the use of genetic science and database technology.

Families must be kept at the center of the search process. Determining the fate and whereabouts of all missing persons requires families' participation in all the steps that impact their rights. This is a part of the victim-centered approach that is inclusive of families and is guided by the ethical principle, of "Do No Harm". All stakeholders want justice for those who are missing and to ensure that this issue is addressed in the framework of transitional justice as well.

Families who that been searching for years or decades have an enormous amount of data on that specific incident when their loved ones went missing. Those data banks include names, coordinates, dates, and other information about these incidents. Building trust with families will require truth and transparency. Being clear with families, careful not to give false hope, but honest in the findings, will establish a connection of trust. These families have been through a lot. For more than a decade, there were very few people they could trust to help them. Now is the time.

Mass Graves

Since the fall of the Assad regime in December 2024, burial sites and mass graves have emerged across Syria attributed to the rule of both Bashar al-Assad and his father, Hafez. Twenty-three miles north of Damascus, located in al-Qutayfah, a primary burial site was discovered. Investigators estimated the mass grave contained the human remains of at least 100,000 people who had been systematically and extrajudicially killed. The Damas al-Qutayfah mass grave site emerged as the most substantial discovery by quantity. The site has been characterized by investigators as a centralized burial location for the regime.

The mass grave was uncovered by non-governmental organizations and several academic researchers associated with the NIOD Institute for War, Holocaust, and Genocide Studies, and the University of Amsterdam. University of Amsterdam genocide studies professor Ugur Umit Ungor, described the site as "a reflection of the killing machine of the Assad regime." Syrian Air Force Intelligence was identified as the primary organization responsible for transporting deceased individuals from detention centers, prisons, or medical facilities to burial sites.

Local witnesses reported seeing security forces transporting bodies in refrigerated containers throughout the Syrian civil war. Religious leader Abdul Kadir al-Sheikha provided testimony about conducting burial rites for at least one hundred victims within a three-hundred-square-foot area before being excluded from future ceremonies by the secret police.

The International Commission on Missing Persons2, in The Hague, reported the existence of at least sixty-six mass grave sites across Syria. Organizations including the Syrian Observatory for Human Rights documented approximately 80,000 confirmed deaths among the missing, with an additional 70,000 individuals believed to have died from torture.

In the settlement of Najha in the southern Damascus countryside, a second large mass grave was discovered. International experts assessed many tens of thousands of human remains were buried in the mass grave. The site is close to an existing cemetery. Investigators discovered that some victims were buried beneath previously established graves. Surface level examinations revealed exposed human remains, including vertebrae and femur fragments.

In Tadamon, investigators discovered a mass grave connected with the Tadamon massacre in April 2013 that held as many as two hundred eighty-eight victims. Additional human remains were spread throughout the area with marks consistent with execution-style killings. Spatial analysis of the grave revealed it measures ten feet by twenty-three feet, with a depth of six feet. The site appeared to be machine-excavated. Investigators collected primary video evidence indicating the execution of forty-one individuals during a single incident. Eleven of the victims were blindfolded and executed at close range. The video shows the victims being pushed into the pre-dug grave, alongside thirteen other bodies. Evidence revealed the mass grave included seven women and twelve children.

Investigators discovered multiple burial sites within a walled-off area, in the Damascus suburb of Adra. Humanitarian teams including the White Helmets recovered skeletal remains in white plastic bags. Preliminary findings indicated at least seven bodies in one location. The teams implemented systematic documentation procedures for collecting genetic DNA samples and preserving evidence for future identification efforts.

Satellite imagery analysis revealed a mass grave site along the road leading to the Damascus International Airport in al-Hussainiyah in the Deir-ez-Zor governorate. Investigators indicated the mass grave contained. approximately twenty victims. Also in the Deir-ez-Zor governate, a mass grave was discovered on 16 December 2024. The newly created site contained the bodies of seventeen Syrian Army soldiers who had been executed.

In the Damascus suburb of Sayyidah Zaynab, the White Helmets uncovered a mass grave on 18 December 2024. The mass grave contained the human remains of at least twenty-one victims. Many of the remains appeared in small pieces or incomplete fragments. The site is located in a predominantly Shia Islam neighborhood close to the Sayyida Zaynab Mosque. The area was a known site for Hezbollah and Iran-backed militia groups before the fall of Assad.

In southern Syria, investigators discovered twelve separate mass graves. One site contained twenty-two victims, including women and children. The victims displayed evidence of torture and execution.

Investigators discovered a mass grave in Mazra' at al-Kuwaiti near Izra on 16 December 2024. The bodies of fifteen, including women and children were burned. The area was previously controlled by a militia linked to the military security branch.

A mass grave was discovered in Qafar, Daraa governorate on 22 December 2024. The site contained the remains of ninety-three victims, including women and children. All of the victims are believed to have been burnt alive according to testimony from a former Military Intelligence officer.

On 25 December 2024, the remains of six victims were found in a field in Umm al Qusur, in the Daraa governate. Investigators indicated the victims were burned and believe dates back more than ten years.

A mass grave containing the skeletal remains and clothing was discovered on 3 January 2025 by residents in southern Syria, in al-Sanamayn near the 9th Division. The remains appeared to have been burned possibly more than a decade ago.

In Homs, a mass grave containing more than 1,200 victims was discovered on 23 December 2024. The victims were detained individuals during the Assad regime, reportedly transferred from the Homs Military Hospital. Also in the Homs governorate, in al-Qadou, three mass graves were discovered on 29 December 2024. The graves contain the remains of twenty persons, believed to have been arrested at military checkpoints during the Assad regime.

A mass grave was discovered in Aleppo on 30 December 2024. Witness testimony indicated that hundreds of detainees were burned at the site.

Two approaches must be applied: protect grave sites and prevent disturbances. In exhumation, attention to collecting evidence is vital to identifying victims, returning the remains to the family, and laying the groundwork for criminal accountability and other judicial processes. Premature exhumations that cannot be carried out to forensic standards may lead to a loss of evidence and contamination of evidence, which can interfere with any future prosecutions.

Response

In January 2025, the transitional president Ahmed al-Shar'aa, pledged to prosecute those responsible for the atrocities committed under Assad's rule in Syria. Al-Shar'aa requested UN assistance in documenting the Assad regime's crimes and emphasized the administration's commitment to justice. Under al-Shar'aa's leadership, the government established a hotline for citizens and former prisoners to report locations of secret prisons and potential burial sites.

In response, NGOs urged authorities to protect mass graves and places of detention so that evidence can be gathered systematically and to a standard that will make it possible to present this evidence at future war crimes trials. Furthermore, genocide studies experts recommended establishing a DNA repository to assist in identifying victims and providing closure for affected families.

Former US war crimes ambassador Stephen Rapp, who led several prosecutions at war crimes tribunals in Rwanda and Sierra Leone, stated that by the number of burial sites, the magnitude of state-sponsored systematic killings had not been witnessed since the Nazis.

In response, the United Nations established three independent panels to determine the status of the missing, as well as address the concerns of the families; the collection of evidence; and investigate human rights violations in Syria.

First, the Independent Institution on Missing Persons in Syria (IIMP) works to clarify the fate and whereabouts of all missing persons in Syria and to provide support to victims, survivors, and their families. IIMP is guided by the ethical principles of "Do No Harm", impartiality, transparency, and the confidentiality of sources and information. The IIMP can, among other measures, support the efforts of the Syrian civil society. The engagement of civil society, including a recognized and active role for families of the missing, can connect political differences and must be based on finding all missing persons and securing the rights of all families, regardless of ethnic or religious affiliation, gender, or role in the conflict. States housing Syrian refugees should be encouraged to support civil society organizations working in the Syrian Diaspora3, and support should be given to Syrian human rights groups and first responders already operating inside Syria.

Second, the International, Impartial, and Independent Mechanism for Syria (IIIM) works to collect evidence, aiming to ensure that those responsible are eventually held accountable. Lastly, the Independent

International Commission on Inquiry on the Syrian Arab Republic (The Commission), works to investigate all alleged violations of international human rights law in Syria since March 2011 and to present public reports on its findings. The Commission reports directly to the Human Rights Council in Geneva.

With the support of international experts, including forensic anthropologists and archeologists, the next step would be to conduct judicial investigations in all cases, collecting and collating verifiable information on crimes and crime scenes, perpetrators, and victims. An integrated and collated data system must be created so that data on missing persons and sites of forensic interests, including mass graves, can be verified and used to help Syria create a Central Record of all missing persons.

These steps will be supported if international organizations pool their expertise and resources and agree on a missing-person assistance plan that can be presented to the Syrian government.

The International Commission on Missing Persons (ICMP) in The Hague has been building the foundation for a comprehensive missing person program in Syria since 2018. ICMP reports that it has already collected data from almost 80,000 relatives who have reported almost 30,000 missing persons. Data, including genetic (DNA) reference samples, has been collected from the Syrian Diaspora and from those areas of Syria that were not under the control of the Assad regime. The opportunity now exists to extend this program across the country.

The Stories

"We all have someone missing." In Syria, it is impossible not to know someone who either has a family member or members missing. The families of the missing share their stories with everyone, hoping that someone can help them find their loved one.

In 2012, the Assad regime cut electricity and water from the city of Homs. Fatima said her husband and son left one evening after the shelling had subsided to look for food and water. They never came back. A few days later, Fatima learned that both were arrested by Assad's security forces and taken into custody to Sednaya. While Fatima and her remaining children survived the war, she learned in December 2024, after the liberation that both her husband and son were disappeared.

American, Austin Tice was working as a freelance journalist in Syria in 2012. He was abducted from a checkpoint in Darayya. In late 2012, a video of a blindfolded Tice was released. It was believed at that time that Tice was being held by the Assad government or its allies. No one has seen or heard from Austin Tice since then. Up to the fall of Assad, the Syrian government repeatedly denied having Tice. However, in the many talks the US State Department has had with Syrian authorities, no one has been able to negotiate his release. He, like so many Syrians, has been disappeared.

In 2013, military services invaded Noor's home in the middle of the night and took every male in her family including her grandfather, father, uncle, and two brothers. As Noor told me the story, I was reminded of Pinochet's DINA in Chile and the Caravan of Death. Noor was seven years old at the time. She believes they were taken to Sednaya. After the prison was liberated and all the prisoners were released, she hoped that she would see her family again, but she has not been able to locate them. She said it was as if they just vanished.

In 2014, Syrian Air Force Security raided the home of the Mousa family. Security forces arrested fourteen people during the raid, including their daughter, Aya, and her two small daughters, Sharma and Isha, ages four and five. The parents were told the three were taken to detention, but they later learned the two granddaughters were taken to Lahn al-Hayat Orphanage. They went to the orphanage, but they were told the girls were not there. They do not know what happened to their family.

After Gaddafi's fall, traffickers exploiting the chaos and taking advantage of the desperation, began smuggling migrants across the perilous 186-mile trip across the Mediterranean Sea between Tripoli, Libya, and Italy. In August 2014, 170 Syrians disappeared when the smuggler's boat capsized in the water. while trying to cross the Mediterranean from Libya to Italy. Their fate remains unknown, they are presumed to have drowned.

In 2015, Mustafa was detained while walking home from work on the street in Damascus by Assad's secret police. He was disappeared. His daughter has tried to find her father who has been missing for nearly a decade. In Damascus, thousands of people search for family members. They post photos of their loved ones hoping to find anyone who might know their whereabouts.

Fadi, Jamil, and Fares were childhood friends in Hama. In 2017, they joined the opposition in the fight against Assad. Jamil's sister Layla said the three left her house to meet some members of the group. She saw them get into a vehicle and leave and they never returned. Layla and her parents tried to find out what happened to them. They filed missing persons reports with the authorities, but nothing ever happened. Layla said she hoped they would show up now that Assad is gone. Her family still has hope.

Countering False Information

Unfortunately, certain individuals or groups may sometimes exploit the suffering of families of missing persons to extract bribes based on false promises of release or information about loved ones, their fate, or whereabouts. Such individuals may impersonate or falsely claim to represent organizations or governments for such purposes. Legitimate organizations and their representatives will never request a fee for their work. Victims and their families can and should contact the organization directly and verify the information. If you have any doubts, or have information about false representation, contact the organization, agency, or government directly.

Many family members have reported receiving notifications from members of the former regime offering to provide them with alleged information on the whereabouts of their loved ones in exchange for significant sums of money. All of these offers have proved to be fraudulent tricks, preying on the emotions and desperation of people to find their missing loved ones. There has also been a network of persons with links to the authorities selling information regarding the whereabouts or deaths of relatives and missing family members.

Bilal from Homs, whose three brothers were abducted in 2012 borrowed more than $150,000 to pay extortionists for information about his brothers. The information was false. In a phone interview, Bilal said the person who contacted him knew his brother's name and when they were abducted. He also knew the circumstances. He said that at the moment, it was not hard to believe the story. But after it was over, he realized the individual could have gotten the information from many sources because Bilal had posted missing fliers everywhere, and on electronic message boards.

Most of the offers are from Syrian secret services and other security circles. The only purpose of their alleged information is to defraud relatives of missing persons.

Amnar Ghouzi said a person close to the regime offered him information about his father's whereabouts for $50,000. He was to pay $20,000 in advance and the rest after obtaining the information. On the advice of relatives and experts, he turned down the offer. Amnar appealed to the German Foreign Office for support as his father is a German national, which obligates the German ministry to make appropriate inquiries. The German authorities said they will look into the case. But again, nothing has happened so far. Ammar has now taken it upon himself to search for his father. He has not given up hope of finding him alive.

Notes

---

[1] International Humanitarian Law (IHL) is a set of policies that work to limit the effect of conflict on civilians. IHL protects civilians who are not involved in the conflict or are victims of the conflict.

[2] The International Commission on Missing Persons (ICMP) is an intergovernmental organization that helps locate missing people. Established by US President Bill Clinton in 1996 at the G-7 Summit in Lyon, France, The organization focuses on armed conflicts, human rights abuses, disasters, organized crimes, and irregular migration. ICMP works with governments, civil society, and families to address the issue of missing people. ICMP assists governments in exhuming mass graves, and helps identify people through DNA analysis, supports family associations of missing people, helps create strategies and institutions to search for missing persons. ICMP speaks from experience it has worked in more than forty countries most notably in the Western Balkans, where more than seventy-five percent of the 40,000 missing persons from the conflicts of the 1990s have been accounted for, including more than ninety percent of the 8,000 men and boys massacred in the Srebrenica Genocide of 1995.https://icmp.int/

[3] Syrian Diaspora refers to the population of Syrian people and their descendants who live outside of Syria having emigrated from the country and now are residing in other parts of the world primarily due to the Syrian Civil War which forced more than six million Syrians to flee as refugees essentially; it is the community of Syrians living abroad.

Chapter Six
The Fall of Assad

In the last three years of the war, the humanitarian crisis in Syria was compounded by an economic collapse triggered by sanctions, and the Covid pandemic. Since 2022, the cost of living has tripled. An earthquake in 2023 further worsened an already catastrophic situation. The country's infrastructure had been decimated by constant shelling and fighting. Syrian currency lost eighty percent of its value and inflation increased to one-hundred-twenty percent by the fall of the regime. By the end of 2024, the poverty rate was over ninety percent. The prolonged instability of the country led to a total collapse of the economy. Most Syrians live on less than $2.15 a day.

In 2011, the United States, the European Union, and most of the Arab League countries called for Assad to resign. He refused and instead increased the brutal crackdowns on the people. Immediately, Syrian activists began using their cell phones to video record the brutal suppressions by the regime, including beatings, the shelling of civilian centers, and indiscriminately firing live rounds at civilians. The brave first responders, the White Helmets, rushed into bombed buildings digging out bodies from rubble. Those early videos uploaded to social media invited the world to witness the atrocities that were being committed by Syria's leadership. They also begged for someone to stop it.

Between 2011 and 2024 over 600,000 people were killed in Syria. According to the Syrian Network for Human Rights, pro-Assad forces caused more than ninety percent of civilian deaths. In 2013, the UN High Commissioner for Human Rights stated that findings from a UN inquiry directly implicated Assad in heinous atrocities and "crimes against humanity."

The Assad government perpetrated numerous war crimes during the war. Assad's Syrian Arab Army forces carried out multiple attacks with banned chemical weapons. The deadliest chemical attack was a sarin gas attack in Ghouta on 21 August 2013 that killed nearly 1,500 people, the majority of whom were women and children. Assad's war crimes led to international condemnation and isolation against his regime.

Nine rounds of UN-mediated peace talks failed to make progress toward peace. Unwilling to step aside, or negotiate with groups, Assad seemed to be more interested in destroying his country than doing what was best for it.

The End of Assad Tyranny

As violence flared up again in Syria in late 2024, the US, Germany, France, and the UK urged for de-escalation in the fighting. A combined effort by rebel groups, led by Hay'at Tahrir al-Sham, had taken control of Aleppo prompting a retaliatory airstrike campaign by Assad and his Russian allies. The strikes, which targeted population centers and several hospitals in the rebel-held city of Idlib, resulted in at least twenty-five deaths.

NATO countries issued a joint statement and called for the protection of civilians and critical infrastructure to prevent further displacement and ensure humanitarian access. They stressed the urgent need for a Syrian-led political solution under UN Security Council Resolution 22541, which advocates for dialogue between the Syrian government and opposition forces. The rebel offensive, which began on 27 November 2024, continued its advance into the Hama governorate following its capture of Aleppo.

Violent clashes erupted in Hama on 4 December, as the Syrian Army engaged rebel insurgents in an attempt to stop their advance on the key city. Government forces claimed to have launched a counter-offensive with air support, pushing back rebels, capturing Hama on 5 December. The fighting led to widespread displacement, with 50,000 people fleeing the area and over 600 casualties, including 104 civilians. However, the rebel forces pushed on, encircling the capital of Damascus and capturing it on 6 December, capturing the strategic city of Homs on 7 December, and cutting off Damascus from regime strongholds on the coast. In the early morning hours of 8 December, the Assad regime collapsed during a major offensive by opposition forces. The offensive was led by Hay'at Tahir al-Sham (HTS) and supported by the Turkish-backed Syrian National Army.

The capture of Homs and Damascus granted opposition forces control over critical transportation infrastructures, particularly the highway junction connecting Damascus to the Alawite coastal region where Assad's support base and the Russian military installations were situated. Assad-allied Hezbollah forces withdrew from al-Qusay. The reduction in support from key allies, including Russia's diminished support due to its war on Ukraine, and Hezbollah's current conflict with Israel, were the driving forces behind Assad's weakened position.

Just before Damascus fell to the rebel forces, Assad fled to Moscow and was granted political asylum by the Russian government. The Russian government said that Assad had "stepped down" as president following a personal decision and had left Syria. Following efforts by Russian foreign minister Sergey Lavrov to facilitate his departure, Assad, who left under great secrecy, was reported to have gone first to the Russian-operated Khmeimin Air Base near Latakia before proceeding to Moscow.

With the fall of Damascus Syrian Prime Minister Mohammed Ghazi al-Jalali handed over power to the revolutionaries. HTS took control of all media and broadcast outlets. Counter-government forces ceased. Al-Jalali remained in Damascus and agreed to cooperate with the new leadership. News of the rapid collapse of the Assad regime was met with shock but also celebrated around the world. It was over. The fall of Bashar al-Assad ended a half-century of Assad family rule.

What is next for Syria

Syria is under new management. The collapse of Assad is the end of the old order. Syria was liberated. The country now has a transitional government – which faces monumental political and economic challenges as well as a devastating humanitarian crisis. For Syrians, the hard work starts now. For the many who survived Assad, they must now find common ground with new leadership, and rebuild their country. And it will not be easy. Much of the country is bombed out... destroyed. Infrastructure is severely damaged. The economy is in ruins. There are still many millions displaced and many hundreds of thousands missing.

But there is a plan to rebuild the country. The blueprint for a transitional government pivot in Syria already exists and is detailed in the UN Security Council Resolution 2254. The blueprint would offer tangible help to Syrians, address pressing challenges, and increase the odds that the transition will succeed. Syria has the potential to become the successful rock of the Arab Spring, that none of the others have seemed to pull off – even if it is thirteen years later.

HTS leader and Syria's transitional President Ahmed al-Shar'aa revealed that public institutions would be temporarily managed by Syrian Prime Minister Mohammad Ghazi al-Jalali until the full political transition was completed. Al-Jalali expressed hope for Syria to become "a normal country" and to be able to engage in diplomacy with other nations.

HTS promised a new Syria where everyone lived in "peace, and justice prevails." The transitional government specifically addressed the displaced population, the Syrian Diaspora, and former political prisoners, and invited everyone to return to Syria. For the Syrian Diaspora, the UN Refugee Agency (UNHCR) has said now that Assad is gone, as many as one million refugees may return to Syria within the first six months of 2025. Several European countries – including Germany and Austria – have said that since Assad has fallen, they will no longer accept asylum applications from Syrian refugees, because there is no threat. The question will be whether Syria's economy can support one million returning refugees.

Mohammed al-Bashir was appointed the new Prime Minister of the Syrian transitional government. HTS said it would protect and allow Christians and other minorities to freely practice their religions, and so far has promised equal rights to all Syrians, as well as decentralization, and regional autonomy. And since Assad's departure led the Syrian Arab Army command to dissolve the military – HTS promised amnesty for Assad's soldiers.

However, there are concerns regarding Ahmad al-Shar'aa. Born in Syria in 1982, Shar'aa is also known as Abu Mohammad al-Jolani. He joined foreign fighters in Iraq in 2003. In 2011 the leader of ISIS, Abu Bakr al-Baghdadi, sent al-Shar'aa to Syria to establish Al-Nusra Front, a branch of Al Qaeda. In 2017, Shar'aa broke ties with al-Qaeda to form Hay'at Tahrir al-Sham (HTS).

HTS is currently designated a terrorist group by the UN, the US, the UK, Canada, and the EU, as well as other countries, although Shar'aa has claimed that he renounced his former extremist beliefs and is a moderate now. Whether that is true remains to be seen as he leads Syria in the transition. Shar'aa has presented himself as a more compassionate and skilled statesman for all Syrians. However, at one time there was a pending $10 million bounty for his capture by the US.

Removing HTS from the designated terrorist list is a good place to start to ensure Syria's success. Easing sanctions against Syria to allow an inflow of funds to ease the suffering of millions would be a good move. Providing support for reconstruction efforts could help Syria rebuild. Although many will say "It is not our problem" a transition that fails and results in renewed violence, and displacement and destabilizes the region further would be more of a problem later.

The US position in all of this: Secretary of State Antony Blinken in the Biden administration said that the US will recognize a Syrian government providing it adheres to four principles: it respects the rights of minorities; facilitates the flow of humanitarian assistance; prevents Syria from being used as a base for terrorism, or poses a threat to its neighbors; and lastly, ensures that chemical weapons are secured and safely destroyed. It is too early to tell what Trump will do.

In a post-Assad world, there are both internal and external interests at play in shaping Syria's future. Syria is divided by competing ethnic and sectarian communities. Which is to say there are many flavors of Islamists in Syria, and each creates barriers to coalition building that could foster greater stability outside of authoritarian rule.

The Syrian rebel groups, for example, have distinct ideologies and priorities and are not necessarily on the same page. HTS is one of four groups that played a role in the ousting of Assad. Besides HTS, there is the Southern Front and the Syrian National Army (SNA) backed by Türkiye, and the Kurdish-led Syrian Democratic Forces (SDF) which is a US partner2 force that defeated ISIS. HTS marched on Damascus, and the predominately Kurdish Syrian Democratic Forces (SDF) expelled the Syrian regime from Qamishli and Al-Hasakah. However, there is still a lot of infighting among the rebel groups. SNA3 guided by Türkiye, has targeted US partner SDF. This Turkish-Kurdish conflict is playing out now in Syria, and it risks undermining everything that has been achieved since the defeat of ISIS. It could jeopardize the historic opportunity to forge a new path for Syria.

How Sunni majority HTS consolidates its authority, and opens civil rights for Shia groups will be the challenge. However, if an Islamist coalition led by HTS can consolidate power in this environment, it would represent a massive transformation in a nation that has long been cursed with instability and indicate significant implications for the region.

Outside Forces to Watch

Israeli Defense Forces initiated military operations in Syria's Quneitra governorate with armored units advancing into the buffer zone between Israeli-controlled Golan Heights and Syria. Prime Minister Benjamin Netanyahu relayed that since the Syrian government had dissolved, then the 1974 border agreement had dissolved as well. IDF carried out airstrikes in Syria, targeting the Mezzeh district of Damascus, in what Netanyahu called suspected chemical weapons storage. He said to avoid any future threat, and until an agreement can be reached with the new Syrian government, Israel would seize the buffer zone. But Netanyahu has already used a hyperbolic thesis to seize control of territory in his ordered dissemination of Gaza and there are signed agreements there as well. What is more likely is that Netanyahu is taking advantage of a moment in time and making a play for another illegal occupation.

However, Israel may find that radical Sunni Islamists are just as dangerous and committed as the Shia Houthi and Hezbollah. Both of

Israel's respective borders are about fifty miles long. However, there is no UN Security Council-mandated buffer zone in Syria, as Resolution 17014 provides in Lebanon. Furthermore, only the United States recognizes Israel's sovereignty in the Golan Heights, which is internationally recognized as Syrian territory. UN Security Council Resolution 4975 explicitly states that Israel's "decision to impose its laws, jurisdiction, and administration in the occupied Golan Heights is null and void without international legal effect."

The main backers of the Assad regime were Iran and Russia. One reason for the rapid collapse was Russia's distraction from the war it started in Ukraine. Concurrently, Iran is facing its own regional challenges. Their inability to come to Assad's aid weakened other conflicts and centers of control. For example, the Houthis in Yemen, Shia militias in Iraq, and Hezbollah in Lebanon. Al-Shar'aa condemned Iran's involvement throughout the war and said Syria would no longer participate in sectarianism and corruption.

Assad's end also means the end of Russian influence in Syria. Of course, Russia is now trying to convince HTS of all the reasons why it should allow Russia to hold on to its air bases. When HTS began its offensive in November, all the groups that fought on Syria's behalf could not scramble fast enough. This is why Bashar al-Assad, and his family, are now living under asylum in Russia.

This new Syria experiment: can shared powers be cohesively knit together equitably and hold – without external actors' meddling offensives from taking it apart? For the sake and security of the Syrian people, let us hope so.

Holding Assad Accountable

There is no shortage of crimes for which to charge Bashar al-Assad in Syria. The mounting evidence of war crimes from arbitrary arrests and detainments to the conditions of cells that humans were subjected to, to the beatings, rapes, starvations, indiscriminate bombings, torture, chemical attacks, the mass executions, to the mass graves that consume the country, reveals the intolerable suffering inflicted by the regime. There is a litany of crimes that lie in its wake.

A frequent form of brutality was barrel bomb attacks. Barrel bombs were oil drums filled with explosives and metal fragments dropped from helicopters, hitting the ground with such force, that they created massive explosions and flying shrapnel. Barrel bombs destroyed buildings and people.

Barrel bombs were also used for chlorine attacks. Chlorine affects the respiratory system, eyes, and skin. Small amounts of chlorine can irritate, but larger amounts of exposure can result in chemical burns. Inhaling chlorine is worse as it can irritate the airway, and cause choking, and breathing problems. It could lead to noncardiogenic pulmonary edema – fluid on the lungs and can be fatal.

In December 2013, the UN High Commissioner for Human Rights Navi Pillay stated that findings from an inquiry by the UN implicated Assad in war crimes. Investigations by the OPCW-UN Joint Investigation Mechanism (2018) and OPCW-UN IIT (2019) both concluded that the Assad government was responsible for the 2017 Khan Shaykhun sarin attack and the 2018 Douma chemical attack. Both of which are war crimes.

Assad also used starvation as a weapon of war by laying complete siege on Homs, Aleppo, and eastern Ghouta, restricting or refusing humanitarian aid to enter. Starvation as a weapon is where governments withhold and control food, or block aid as a means to manage their citizens. Armed groups use the promise of the next meal as a psychological means to force entire communities of civilians to participate in the conflict. Since the start of the war, the regime made the use of starvation as a weapon, habitual. Crop burning, bombing fields, and food storage facilities, sealing off besieged areas, and denying access to food, water, medical supplies, and other aid, have been regular offenses of Assad.

Up to this point, Assad has been protected from prosecution under immunity in his role as president. But all of that ended on 8 December 2024. So will he be held accountable, and if so what does that look like?

Several legal obstacles stand in the way of criminal accountability. The International Criminal Court in The Hague is the most obvious choice for prosecuting Assad. However, the ICC does not have jurisdiction over Syria, since the country is not a signatory to the Rome Statute6 – the government treaty of the Court.

The new leadership in Syria could ratify the treaty and grant the Court jurisdiction and retroactive jurisdiction, which would allow the prosecutor to examine cases from previous years. But that would also bring any crimes the new government and rebel forces committed to light, and they could be charged as well.

The UN Security Council could refer a case to the ICC, granting it jurisdiction. However, Russia and China have blocked such votes repeatedly. Given its alliance with Assad, any vote would certainly be vetoed by Russia, especially considering its own complicity in the crimes. When Russia joined the war to support Assad, it provided air support to attack hospitals, schools, apartment buildings, and other civilian centers – all considered war crimes.

Most of the members of the government especially those involved with military activities, fled the country, many believe they are in Russia or Iran. The list of fugitives is long. Those at large include Minister of Defense Ali Mahmoud Abbas, Minister of the Interior Mohammad Khaled-al Rahmoun, Chief of the General Staff Abdul Karim Mahmoud Ibrahim, and the head of the National Security Office Kifah Moulhem. And of course, the entire Assad family. It is doubtful that either country will hand anyone over.

There is another option. The ICC could use jurisdictional leverage over a member state to force the referral. For example, if the Court used leverage against Jordan because it forcibly expelled Syrians across its border back to a war zone, which is a violation of international humanitarian law. While there is a precedent for this, it is not likely to happen.

Individual courts inside and outside of Syria could bring charges, and we have seen this happening in other countries. Universal jurisdiction allows non-Syrian courts to prosecute Syrians for crimes against humanity, war crimes, and torture. Criminal cases against regime officers have already been filed in French, German, Austrian, Norwegian, Swedish, and US courts.

Judicial authorities in France issued an arrest warrant for al-Assad on 20 January 2025, for suspected complicity in war crimes stemming from an attack on civilians in Deraa, Syria, in 2017. Franco-Syrian national, Salah Abou Nabout was killed in the attack. An investigation into the death was opened in 2018, at which time judges issued arrest warrants for six high-ranking Syrian army officials, believed to be following Assad's orders. This is the second time France has issued arrest warrants for Al-Assad. The first, in November 2023, a French court issued an international arrest warrant for Bashar al-Assad, his brother, and two officials over an attack against civilians using chemical weapons in 2013. More than one thousand people were killed, mostly women and children.

On 9 December 2024, an indictment was unsealed in the Northern District of Illinois charging two former Syrian Air Force Intelligence officers, Abdul Salam Mahmoud and Jamil Hassan with conspiracy to commit war crimes through the infliction of cruel and inhumane treatment on detainees under their control, including US citizens.

On 8 June 2023, Canada and the Netherlands jointly initiated proceedings against Syria before the International Court of Justice (ICJ) concerning alleged violations of the Convention against Torture and Other Cruel, Inhuman or Degrading Treatment or Punishment. On 16 November 2023, the ICJ issued provisional measures calling on the government of Syria to prevent acts of torture and other cruel, inhuman, or degrading treatment or punishment, ensure its officials do not commit any acts of torture, and guarantee the preservation of relevant evidence.

In 2020, German courts prosecuted two former high-level Syrian officials. One of them was found guilty of crimes against humanity and sentenced to life in prison.

The ICC is exploring how to ensure accountability for crimes committed under the Assad regime. ICC Chief Prosecutor Karim Khan met with Syria's new leader Ahmed al-Shar'aa on how to ensure accountability for crimes committed under the Assad regime.

Transitional President Ahmed al-Shar'aa has vowed to pursue the regime's collaborators in Syria and has called on countries to hand over those who fled, so justice can be served. But it is too early to tell if the transitional government will ensure any Syrian criminal proceedings are carried out. At this time, we do not know what the future state of Syria will look like. We cannot see how the institutions will function, and cooperate. An ideal option would be for Syria to hold trials without attaching the death penalty. There would also need to be guardrails put in place to ensure that witnesses and victims are allowed to give testimonies and be protected.

But it is unlikely that Bashar al-Assad will surrender himself to stand trial in Syria or anywhere else. He no doubt remembers what the people of Libya did to Gaddafi. It is also inconceivable that neither Moscow nor Iran will hand anyone over. There is nothing in it for them.

Other efforts to hold Assad and Syrian officials accountable have included visa bans, sanctions, and the freezing of Syrian assets by various governments including Canada, Australia, the UK, and the EU. In 2012 and 2020, the US imposed sanctions under the Global Magnitsky Act and the Caesar Syria Civilian Act.

We all hope that one day there will be a shift in geopolitical conditions and Assad and all of those who committed atrocities in Syria will be held accountable. However, none of that is possible without the evidence to prove a case.

Preserving the evidence is critical to any future prosecution and the ability to hold the perpetrators accountable. Securing the evidence prevents the more perverse risk that other actors could confiscate evidence for political purposes, or that evidence could be destroyed to prevent prosecution. During the rebels' offensive, there were missing computers, damaged computers, hard drives that were burned and smashed, and files thrown about. In the initial days, there were exhumations carried out without forensic teams. These actions destroy evidence and are an obstacle to bringing the perpetrators to justice.

Notes

[1] UN Security Council Resolution 2254 – calls on the parties to immediately allow humanitarian agencies rapid, sage, and unhindered access throughout Syria by most direct routes. The resolution calls for a ceasefire and political settlement, and endorses a road map for the peace process in Syria.
https://www.securitycouncilreport.org/atf/cf/%7B65BFCF9B-6D27-4E9C-8CD3-CF6E4FF96FF9%7D/s_res_2254.pdf

[2] There were a fair number of Kurds who were actually with the uprising in the beginning, particularly when it was a peaceful protest. The Kurds, also known as the People's Defense Unit, or YPG, is a libertarian socialist, US-backed Kurdish militant group in Syria and the primary component of the Syrian Democratic Forces (SDP). They defeated ISIS in Kobani in 2015 and liberated Raqqa in 2017. The US airdropped weapons and support to them. But because of its association with PKK, Türkiye and Qatar have designated YPK as a terrorist organization. But in 2019, they were the most effective force in the fight against the Islamic State.

[3] Syrians suffer from hostilities and unrest along multiple regional frontlines, including across northeast Syria. In northwest Syria, including the Idlib governorate, ground fighting, shelling, and airstrikes have continued despite a ceasefire that has been in place since March 2020. Elsewhere in northern Syria, hostilities and strikes between the SNA and Syrian Defense Forces (SDF) have escalated. Improvised explosive devices, indiscriminate shelling, and airstrikes killed and wounded hundreds of civilians through 2023

[4] UN Security Council Resolution 1701 was passed in 2006 to end hostilities between Israel and Hezbollah. The resolution established a UN peacekeeping force in Lebanon to monitor the ceasefire and ensure the safe return of displaced people. https://docs.un.org/en/S/RES/1701(2006)

[5] UN Security Council Resolution 497 was a unanimous resolution adopted in 1981 that condemned Israel's annexation of the Golan Heights. The resolution called on Israel to reverse the annexation. It declared that the Israeli annexation of the Golan Heights was "null and void and without international legal effect." The resolution called on Israel to rescind its decision to impose its laws in the Golan Heights. It determined that the Geneva Convention of 1949 on the Protection of Civilian Persons in Time of War still applied ot the Golan Heights. It requested the UN Secretary-General to report back on the resolution's implementation within two weeks. It stated that the Security Council

would meet again by 5 January 1982 to consider further action if Israel did not comply. Israel did not comply with the resolution. The US vetoed a resolution that would have called for international action against Israel. A special session of the UN General Assembly called for a boycott of Israel.   https://docs.un.org/S/RES/497(1981)

[6] The Rome Statute of the International Criminal Court is an international treaty that established the Court. The statute defines the court's jurisdiction, procedures, and cooperation obligations. The Rome Statute was adopted in Rome on 17 July 1998 and went into effect on 1 July 2002. The statute covers crimes such as genocide, war crimes, crimes against humanity, and aggression. The statute establishes the court's structure, including the composition, administration, and independence of the judges. The statute also addresses issues such as admissibility, applicable law, investigations, prosecutions, and appeals.   https://www.thegenocidereport.org/rome-statute-of-the-international-criminal-court/

Chapter Seven
Making the World a Witness

When I was younger, if I had a bad dream or a nightmare, it was usually of snakes. To this day, I am terrified of snakes. But my night terrors are no longer of that – but of something much worse. It is the job of parents to protect their children, comfort them, and console them when they have bad dreams. Children in conflict experience things that no child should ever have to face – or be forced to remember for the rest of their lives.

In war zones, parents go to bed at night with the fear that their children may not live to see the morning. To the vast majority of the world's population, that is incomprehensible. What role do children have in war, except to die? These are questions heard frequently from parents, humanitarian workers, and medical staff, even from our team, in the field. I do not know why the war machine targets the most vulnerable. Assad claimed that he was bombing terrorists and yet there are countless videos and photos to show the majority of people he killed were women and children.

When Bashar al-Assad was a child, he watched his father, Hafez, crush the opposition by shelling cities into submission and ruins, killing tens of thousands of civilians. And he watched him do it with impunity. So, why would Bashar not think he could do the same?

Assad targeted women and children. He starved them to death. He commanded his forces to bomb them to death. He ordered men and boys to be rounded up and imprisoned, and he tortured them to death or hanged them in mass executions. At no time did he consider the sorrow of his people. A medical doctor, who took an oath to "Do No Harm"1. And yet, he did those things. And he did them for twenty-four years. Now that he has fled to Russia - it appears he also carried out all those atrocities with impunity.

Assad failed to unite his people. He had an opportunity to be the reform leader – to turn the page to a better Syria, a brighter Syria. Now, all he will ever be remembered for are his brutalities, his war crimes, and his failures as a leader. The Assad name is forever etched in history as a family that terrorized the people without remorse.

In the course of my career, I have had several opportunities to visit Syria, with various agencies and organizations, some for humanitarian purposes and others for investigative reasons. My first trip was in 2012. I was taken aback by the level of destruction, and overwhelmed by the number of displaced persons and the massive amount of need. Syria was different from Yemen. For me, Syria came first.

Resistance comes in many forms. Having witnessed a few of the peaceful protests in Syria, though I did not participate, I have a great amount of respect for the people who risked their lives just to show up and chant, "Peaceful, Peaceful" and "We want change" knowing that they were going to be attacked by Assad's forces. Witnessing the government violently brutalizing the peaceful protesters in the streets of Damascus was unsettling, if not frightening. However, the people continued to resist Assad's tyrannical regime. The demonstrations became more sectarian over time. The majority of Syrians are Sunni and the Assads are from a tiny minority Alawite religious sect, which is Shia. But the more people resisted, in word and action, the more violent the government became. As time went on, violence against protesters was only a small fraction of the crimes Bashar al-Assad inflicted on his people.

But the initial hope that Syrians held, that the protests would lead to immediate political reform, end corruption, and generate economic equity with the resignation of Assad, was extinguished when it became clear that it would take a violent revolution, for Syria to achieve peace. Before there could be peace, the people of Syria, like the people of Libya, Iraq, and Yemen, would have to face the counter-revolution which included state, regional, and international military actors and a destructive civil war, that would last thirteen years.

At the lowest point of the conflict, when it looked like the opposition might be successful in deposing Assad, the regime controlled less than twenty percent of Syria. The ancient city of Palmyra was all but destroyed. The Islamic State got within a few miles of the presidential palace. In the summer of 2012, everyone on the outside looking in was saying it was over. Then-Secretary of State Hillary Clinton said the writing is on the wall. In Geneva, there was a debate over which country was going to take Assad once he was exiled from Syria – whether it would be Latin America or an African country. We thought we were witnessing the end of the regime. And that is when Iran entered the picture.

We witnessed the Iranians provide support when they took the lead in defeating the opposition offensive in Damascus. The Assad regime made a deal with Iran that ensured that the oil-rich region of the north-northeast corner of Syria would be protected. The regime kept the airport in that area and a security presence in the city of Qamishli, in northeast Syria.

At that time, Syrians have been through this extraordinary humanitarian collapse with half the country fully displaced and towns and cities destroyed. Millions of people had fled the country and were living in neighboring countries. With Iran's help, Assad had re-established control over almost all of the country.

Then came the destruction of Homs. Homs became the capital of the rebellion. So, in an attempt to quash the opposition, Assad's forces laid a brutal and complete siege of Homs. There was no electricity, no access to clean water, no humanitarian aid allowed in, no food, no medical supplies. People were starving. Women could not nurse their infants. Children were being gunned down by Assad's snipers. And the airstrikes were constant. The scale of the atrocities grew in intensity, and the world became more aware of what was happening in Syria.

In other parts of Syria, such as Aleppo, people who had been displaced were moving back to where their homes once were, but they had no idea what to expect. The vast majority of civilians did not trust the regime, but many were practical and saw moving back as the only option. They knew that Assad was being defended by Iran and Russia. Since no action was being taken by the US or Europe, the consensus was that anyone who could help – would not. That was the perception on the part of the Syrians. Assad had gassed people, committed massacres, and targeted hospitals, and he and his partners had been doing so for a while, and nobody was going after him. To Syrians, it appeared as if the world was okay with what he was doing.

So the attitude of most Syrians was, "What can we do?" And they reconciled themselves to the fact that there was nothing they could do. They had witnessed what Syrians who left the country had to go through, the indignity, danger, and humiliation, particularly in the region, in countries like Lebanon, Jordan, Türkiye, and also in Europe. They had heard of people getting on rubber rafts and then being lost at sea. So they said, maybe we should just stay home, and take our chances with Assad. One resident of Damascus told me, "There's nothing we can do. It's the same fear that we were living under before. People are being arrested… being disappeared." In a lot of the areas that Assad recovered thanks to Iran and Russia, anyone who was suspected of having protested or taken part in any anti-regime activities was arrested again, and in most cases disappeared. The prisons were filled with civilians – many died in prison.

So there was no prospect of meaningful social stability going forward. On that first trip to Syria, on the last day there, a woman who knew I was American asked me, "How can this be happening? Why is no one helping us?" And I did not know how to respond to that. I will never forget that woman's face. I did not have an answer for her then. Now that I know Assad will likely never have to suffer the consequences for what he did, it bothers me deeply. There has to be some fragment of justice for Syria… for that woman.

Throughout the war, in areas that were under Assad's control, the government systematically perpetrated arbitrary arrests, torture, enforced disappearances, and deaths in detention. In areas that were previously held by the opposition, the government imposed arbitrary restrictions on freedom of movement and deprived individuals of their property, which may amount to collective punishment, which is a war crime.

Meanwhile, armed groups, like the Syrian National Army (SNA) and other Turkish-backed groups, also perpetrated torture, ill-treatment, systematic looting, and arbitrary detention. Notably, the armed group Hay'at Tahrir al-Sham (HTS), which is currently running the transitional government in Syria, also perpetrated abuses, including arbitrarily detaining activists and journalists, and torture and ill-treatment in detention.

For over a decade, the government of Syria, its allies, and armed opposition groups have all perpetrated countless attacks on civilians and civilian infrastructure, blatantly disregarding international law. Government forces have committed murder, torture, and sexual violence as a matter of state policy.

As various armed groups attempted to consolidate their control over territory in a fragmented Syria, civilians faced indiscriminate hostilities, as well as widespread and systematic human rights violations. The Syrian government and other parties to the conflict continued to perpetrate detention and disappearance as a strategy to control and intimidate civilians confirming ongoing patterns of crimes against humanity and war crimes. This is to say that the only way to deal with the civilian population is to lock them up, torture them, and make examples of a few to ensure that the millions stay in line and do not resist.

It is both a fractured country and a fractured society. The only hope we have is that we have meaningful justice and accountability and a process where people who have committed war crimes – the regime and other actors – are held accountable and that they are made to pay for these crimes.

The ideals of accountability and justice made me want to shine a light on the atrocities of war. But it comes at a price. I cared enough to go to these places, in the hope that I could get others to care. But once you have seen these things, you cannot unsee them. Once you know something, you cannot unknow it.

In my career, I have spent a significant amount of time in conflict. I do not enjoy being in a war zone, but I feel compelled to see it for myself so that when I argue these things, I have a valid point of reference. I do not trust the freedoms taken to change the perspectives of the causes of war, conflict, and violence – to reshape realities to suit one side or another. And so I see it for myself in its raw, painful form absorbing all the human suffering in the hope of shedding some light on the issues.

Transparency, accountability, and truth have been removed from political language and war discourse. Representatives from all sides lie and cover the truth with misinformation and disinformation – as camouflage – in part to keep people blinded to what is happening, to keep them from asking questions. But we have to face what war does… we have to face the human horrors and tell people what happens when all sides try to obscure the truth… if for no other reason, than for the sake of humanity. Can we really make a difference? I believe we can. The real difficulty is having enough faith in humanity to believe that enough people will care.

In the many conversations I have with people, advocating for international humanitarian law (IHL) and international human rights to be upheld, I find that there is a never-ending opportunity to impress upon others that IHL is not something a bunch of "bleeding hearts" created to feel good, but that they are the protocols (laws) for how people are supposed to behave in war and how they are supposed to treat civilians.

The origins of international humanitarian law date back to the 1860s. In 1863, Francis Lieber's The Lieber Code was published which outlines detailed rules of warfare. Early IHL was established in 1864 when the Geneva Convention for the Amelioration of the Conditions of the Wounded and Sick in Armed Forces in the Field was adopted. The St. Petersburg Declaration of 1868 banned certain explosives and incendiary ammunition. The First Geneva Convention and other Geneva Conventions were adopted in 1949. In 1977, the Additional Protocols to the Geneva Conventions were adopted, and in 2005, the Third Additional Protocols were adopted. And every single one of these, and more, were suggested, debated, argued over, and finally agreed upon by country leadership – to hold as law. There is no excuse for countries to evade IHL.

The war machine can avoid bombing schools, hospitals, residential areas, and civilian communities – the solution is simply not to do it. That is why we have to tell the stories of the people we meet in places like Yemen, Afghanistan, Gaza, and Syria.

Some people blame the UN... but what is the UN? It is an inter-governmental organization comprised of member states. Who are the members? The members are countries. Policies are derived from the member countries and ultimately controlled by five permanent members of the United Nations Security Council: China, Russia, the United States, France, and the United Kingdom, with the veto power that if one says no... the answer is no. And so there is constant stalemate to prevent wars from ending, aid from being delivered, and leaders and other actors from being held accountable for the atrocities they commit against their people... the ultimate cost of war. For thirteen years, Russia and China blocked any attempt by the UN Security Council to hold Assad accountable and refer the regime to the International Criminal Court. And now that Assad is in Russia... who knows?

But I refuse to believe that evil wins. This story is not over. The fall of Assad ushered in new hope, justice, and a future for Syria. Syria will have peace and freedom. And one day the people of Syria will have justice.

Hannah Ardent said, "Revolutions are the only political events which confront us directly and inevitably with the problem of beginning." Syria's rebirth will be painful, and frustrating. But it can also be a fresh start... If it can cleanse itself of its past.

How You Can Help

People ask me all the time, "What can I do? How can I help? How do I make a difference?"

The most impactful way to help the people of Syria, or anywhere there is conflict, war, or climate emergency, is to donate to organizations that are actively on the ground in the country supporting them. The International Committee of the Red Cross (ICRC), Doctors Without Borders (MSF) International Rescue Committee, and UNHCR – these organizations help provide essential aid to refugees and displaced persons such as food, shelter, and medical care. The people who work with these groups really do care and are committed to helping improve situations, conditions, and the lives of people impacted by unimaginable circumstances.

Becoming a monthly donor – even if you can only give $10 a month – collectively it is a lot, and you are part of a larger group that provides long-term support.

In 2021, when I wrote Stories from Yemen: A Diary from the Field, there were eighty-four million people displaced due to war, conflict and violence, and climate crisis. Today, there are more than one hundred twenty million. Many causes need volunteers. If working in a humanitarian capacity is something that interests you, I cannot think of a better way to begin the experience than volunteering with a local organization that works with resettled refugees. And if you hope to work in the field or with the UN, taking a couple of languages – Spanish, French, and Arabic is a good place to start.

If the area in which you live has a local resettlement office, you can volunteer at the office. People who are new to the area will appreciate a familiar face to help them adjust to the new surroundings. You might be able to teach them the bus routes and how to navigate public transportation.

Be a friend. It costs nothing to be nice. Most people who come from conflict regions around the world – not just Syria – have had a difficult time. Approach them with empathy and compassion, listen to them, and show a genuine interest in their experiences.

Respect the boundaries. Be patient, and understanding, and avoid pressuring them to discuss the details of their experience. Be mindful of sensitive political issues related to the conflict and avoid taking sides.

Focus on common ground, shared interests, and activities that could provide a sense of normalcy and connection. Pay close attention to what they say, ask clarifying questions, and show genuine interest in their perspective.

Offer support. Ask how you can help, whether it is just being a listening ear or connecting them with relevant resources if needed. If they seem to be struggling with significant trauma, encourage them to seek professional support from a therapist or counselor.

Find a cause that aligns with their interests and consider doing volunteer work together. If they are learning a new language, joining a class can be a great way to interact casually.

Use social media or online forums to connect with people from similar backgrounds. Understand the cultural context of their experiences and be respectful of their traditions.

Resist Hate

The only way to counter hate is to call it out. Growing up in the South in the 1960s and 70s, witnessing racism, was my first lesson in hate. To dislike someone because of the color of their skin, or their accent, or their religion, or their language, or their nationality, or, or, or… is such a waste of time and energy, and nothing is ever accomplished by it. My friends know me well enough to know that I do not tolerate hate speech, bigoted viewpoints, prejudice, racism, or xenophobia. And I'm pretty quick to remind people that we are all created in the image of God. And most of the time that shuts people down. But occasionally you get someone whose life is filled with hate. I have never been a very patient person. But as I have grown older, I find I'm still a bit impatient; it is just that the things I'm impatient about have shifted. I'm impatient with meanness, hate, cruelty, and injustice.

You can be the difference. There are also many opportunities in your local community to make a difference. It means a lot to someone who is resettled in your area if you are simply nice to them. And remember that contrary to the latest soundbite on "hate TV" everyone that is in your area from far away is not a terrorist. Everyone who crosses a border is not there to steal your job or prevent you from getting ahead or is a dangerous criminal. Be a friend. Be an advocate. Be an encourager.

I'm grateful to have a compassionate heart... and to be able to do the work I do. The people we meet, want what all of us want... to live in peace. And so I write and speak about these things because it is my way to resist, to protest the horrors of war and its atrocities, and to help an unsuspecting world understand why these things should stop... why peaceful and diplomatic solutions to war and crisis are healthier... are better for the whole of humanity.

In Memoriam

Brad had a laugh that sounded like James Earl Jones. It was larger than life – which is fitting because Brad was larger than life. Brad's entire career as a humanitarian could be summed up as – we go because people are hurting, and they need us to be there.

In August 2012, an aid convoy he was on came under an air assault and Brad suffered burns to eighty-six percent of his body. Although his body healed with time, the trauma he suffered as a result of the assault did not. He struggled with depression and vivid flashbacks that led to excruciating pain. He was tormented by self-blame and guilt because he could not return to the field – he felt he had let everyone down.

I remember sharing something with Brad that someone shared with me when I returned from Yemen. When something bad happens the mind locks the event in the subconscious – which is the place where memories are stored. The subconscious cannot tell the difference between what is real and what is a memory, which is why the flashbacks seem so real – like they are happening in the "now".

Trauma is real and you cannot push it aside or expect it to go away on its own. You have to find a way to deal with the trauma. Brad tried, but after twelve years, he lost the battle and ended his life. Brad was also a casualty of Bashar al-Assad it just took twelve more years for him to die.

Lara Kajs

Humanitarian workers and healthcare professionals often work under dangerous and extreme conditions and are nearly one hundred percent of the time exposed to trauma. You may leave the conflict behind, but that does not mean you leave the trauma behind. You are not alone, please seek help and talk it out.

And to so many men, women, and children in Syria and anywhere there is war, conflict, violence, and displacement, try to find someone, a professional to help you address the concerns. You do not have to experience this on your own.

Notes

[1] The Hippocratic Oath is a historical medical text, considered one of the earliest expressions of medical ethics, where a new physician swears to uphold professional ethical standards, including prioritizing patient well-being, maintaining confidentiality, and "first, do no harm," traditionally invoking Greek gods as witnesses. The principles of the oath: do not kill, do not cause pain and suffering, do not incapacitate, do not cause offense, do not deprive others of the goods of life

About the Author

Lara Kajs is an author, speaker, founder, advocate, and humanitarian. She is the author of Stories from Yemen: A Diary from the Field, and Assad's Syria, and the founder and executive director of The Genocide Report (TGR) an NGO nonprofit in Washington, DC. She is an international expert on atrocity crimes, forced displacement, state terrorism, and International Humanitarian Law. She consults with the UN and the International Criminal Court.

Kajs holds graduate degrees from the University of Tennessee Knoxville, Lincoln Memorial University, and the University of Nevada Las Vegas. She received a BA in Spanish from the University of Hawai'i Manoa. She is a member of Kappa Delta Sorority, the International Society of Female Professionals, the International Association of Genocide Scholars, the International Network of Genocide Scholars, and the American Historical Association.

Kajs was born in Birmingham, Alabama, is a passionate Crimson Tide fan, and an ardent lover of music – one rock band in particular. She has journeyed to more than 140 countries and lived in seven. Kajs resides in Washington, DC.

Visit larakajs.com to learn more about the author and her work. Follow Lara Kajs on Facebook, Instagram, X, and LinkedIn

For speaking and interview inquiries please contact Stephanie Marcum at smarcum@thegenocidereport.org

Index

children… 16,26,30, 33-39, 42-47, 62-67, 70, 94-98, 104-118, 131-137, 141, 152

Chile   83, 111

Clinton Administration   8,31,116,140

crimes against humanity   34,74,118,130,132,135,143

Damascus   v, 11, 12, 17,22, 27,28,73,85,91,102, 112, 121, 139, 140

Daraa   17, 26, 27, 29, 44, 106

Dirty War   83

disappeared…81,97,99,100,111,112,142

displacement…vii, viii,31,40-47,53-58, 60,70,119,124,152,155,163

Egypt   3,4, 15-17, 22, 24-26,32,44, 48,61, 82,

exhumation   101, 107, 133

extermination   75,77,78,96

extraordinary rendition   13. 22. 73

Gaddafi   25, 112, 133

Ghouta   36, 118, 128

Golan Heights   5, 125, 126, 134

Hama 17, 20, 26, 27, 28, 88, 112, 119

Hama Massacre   7, 26

Hamza 29, 30

Hay'at Tahrir al-Sham   39, 119, 123, 143

Hezbollah   32, 35, 39, 105, 120, 126, 127, 134

Homs   9, 17, 18, 33, 34, 37, 38, 85, 106, 107, 110, 114, 120, 126, 140

HTS   39, 94, 120 – 127, 143

Further Reading

Ali, Nujood. I am Nujood, Age 10, and Divorced. New York: Three Rivers Press, 2010.

Avanzini, Alessandra. By Land and Sea: A History of South Arabia before Islam Recounted from Inscriptions. Rome: L'Erma di Bretschneider, 2016.

Aziz, Muhammad Ali. Religion and Mysticism in Early Islam. London: I.B. Tauris, 2011

Bellamy, Alex J. Syria Betrayed: Atrocities, War, and the Failure of International Diplomacy. New York: Columbia University Press, 2022.

Blashfield, Jean F. Yemen. Portsmouth: Heinemann Publishing, 2011.

Blumi, Isa. Chaos in Yemen. New York: Routledge, 2010.

Blumi, Isa. Destroying Yemen: What Chaos in Arabia Tells Us About the World. Berkeley: University of California Press, 2018.

Brandt, Marieke. Tribes and Politics in Yemen: A History of the Houthi Conflict. New York: Oxford University Press, 2017.

Brehony, Noel. Yemen Divided: The Story of a Failed State in South Arabia. London: I.B. Tauris, 2013.

Bryce, Trevor. Ancient Syria: A Three Thousand Year History. London: Oxford, 2014.

Carapico, Sheila. Arabia Incognita: Dispatches from Yemen and the Gulf. Washington: Just World Books, 2016.

Dagher, Sam. Assad or We Burn the Country: How One Family's Lust for Power Destroyed Syria. New York: Back Bay Books, 2020.

Demeter, Daniel, and Joshua Landis. Lens on Syria: A Photographic Tour of Its Ancient and Modern Culture. New York: Just World Books, 2016.

Eggers, Dave. The Monk of Mokha. New York: Vintage, 2019.

Ferris, Jesse. Nasser's Gamble: How Intervention in Yemen Caused the Six-Day War and the Decline of Egyptian Power. Princeton: Princeton University Press, 2015.

Goodwin, Sam. Saving Sam: The True Story of an America's Disappearance in Syria and His Family's Extraordinary Fight to Bring Him Home. New York: Hatchet Book Group, 2024.

Harrower, Michael. Water Histories and Spatial Archaeology. New York: Cambridge University Press, 2016.

Has, Paul. Yemen History, and Civil War. New York: Creative Space, 2016.

Hill, Ginny. Yemen Endures. New York: Oxford University Press, 2017.

Ho, Engseng. The Graves of Tarim. Berkeley: University of California Press, 2006.

Kajs, Lara. Stories from Yemen: A Diary from the Field. Washington: Ingram. 2022.

Kullab, Samya, and Jackie Roche. Escape from Syria. New York: Firefly Books, 2020.

Lackner, Helen. Yemen in Crisis: Road to War. New York: Penguin, 2011.

Lesch, David W. Syria: A Modern History. Cambridge: Polity, 2019.

Malek, Alia. The Home That Was Our Country: A Memoir of Syria. New York: Bold Type Books, 2018.

Muller, Gert. The African Rulers of Medieval Yemen. London: Pomegranate Publisher, 2012.

Najem, Muhammad. Muhammad Najem, War Reporter: How One Boy Put the Spotlight on Syria. New York: Little Brown Ink, 2022.

Orkaby, Asher. Beyond the Arab Cold War: The International History of the Yemen Civil War, 1962 – 68. New York: Oxford University Press, 2019.

Pearlman, Wendy. We Crossed a Bridge and it Trembled: Voices from Syria. New York: Harper Collins, 2018.

Peutz, Nathaniel. Islands of Heritage: Conservation and Transformation in Yemen. Stanford: Stanford University Press, 2018.

Phillips, Christopher. The Battle for Syria: International Rivalry in the New Middle East. New Haven: Yale University Press, 2020.

Phillips, Sarah. Yemen and the Politics of Permanent Crisis. New York: Routledge, 2011.

Reilly, James A. Fragile Nation, Shattered Land: The Modern History of Syria. New York: Lynne Rienner Publishers, Inc., 2021.

Szekely, Ora. Syria Divided: Patterns of Violence in a Complex Civil War (Columbia Studies in Middle East Politics). New York: Columbia University Press, 2023.

Thesiger, Wilfred. Arabian Sands. New York: Penguin, 2008.

Van Dam, Nikolaos. Destroying a Nation: The Civil War in Syria. London: IB Taurus, 2017.

Stories from Yemen: A Diary from the Field

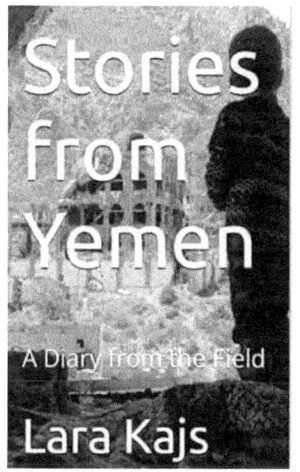

Yemen is a magical place. Its beauty is the land, the diversity of culture, its heritage, and the people. But that beauty has been marred by nearly a decade of conflict; a conflict that has led to the worst humanitarian crisis in recorded history. As author Lara Kajs points out, ignoring the crisis in Yemen will be the loss of humanity and to our detriment.

Stories from Yemen: A Diary from the Field is a first-person account of the humanitarian crisis in Yemen and shares the stories of nearly a hundred Yemeni men, women, and children, and how they have been impacted by the conflict – through displacement, being unhoused, food insecurity, sickness, economic collapse, and concern for the safety and wellbeing of their children, and death. All of this while trying to avoid conflict, airstrikes, bullets, landmines, and traffickers.

Ms. Kajs writes from the perspective of someone who spent seventeen months in Yemen between 2018 and 2021, as a humanitarian observer and crisis investigator, during some of the heaviest fighting and airstrikes – and experienced her own close calls with the conflict. Kajs' clear and impassioned account of the Yemeni people and the plight of the embattled country of Yemen, increasingly engages the reader.

Stories from Yemen: A Diary from the Field is available in E-Book, Paperback, and Hardcover at Amazon, Barnes and Noble, Apple Books, and independent booksellers worldwide. Distributed by Ingram Books.

www.ingramcontent.com/pod-product-compliance
Lightning Source LLC
Chambersburg PA
CBHW071739120626
46550CB00002B/576